ZZ
EC 3
84 A 37

AGRICULTURAL TRADE WITH DEVELOPING COUNTRIES

ORGANISATION FOR ECONOMIC CO-OPERATION AND DEVELOPMENT

Pursuant to article 1 of the Convention signed in Paris on 14th December, 1960, and which came into force on 30th September, 1961, the Organisation for Economic Co-operation and Development (OECD) shall promote policies designed:

- to achieve the highest sustainable economic growth and employment and a rising standard of living in Member countries, while maintaining financial stability, and thus to contribute to the development of the world economy;
- to contribute to sound economic expansion in Member as well as non-member countries in the process of economic development; and
- to contribute to the expansion of world trade on a multilateral, non-discriminatory basis in accordance with international obligations.

The Signatories of the Convention on the OECD are Austria, Belgium, Canada, Denmark, France, the Federal Republic of Germany, Greece, Iceland, Ireland, Italy, Luxembourg, the Netherlands, Norway, Portugal, Spain, Sweden, Switzerland, Turkey, the United Kingdom and the United States. The following countries acceded subsequently to this Convention (the dates are those on which the instruments of accession were deposited): Japan (28th April, 1964), Finland (28th January, 1969), Australia (7th June, 1971) and New Zealand (29th May, 1973).

The Socialist Federal Republic of Yugoslavia takes part in certain work of the OECD (agreement of 28th October, 1961).

Publié en français sous le titre:

ÉCHANGES AGRICOLES
AVEC LES PAYS EN DÉVELOPPEMENT

© OECD, 1984
Application for permission to reproduce or translate
all or part of this publication should be made to:
Director of Information, OECD
2, rue André-Pascal, 75775 PARIS CEDEX 16, France.

This study was carried out by the Joint Working Party of the Committee for Agriculture and the Trade Committee and was approved by both Committees in June 1983. The OECD Council agreed to its publication in September 1983.

Also available

PROBLEMS OF AGRICULTURAL TRADE (October 1982)
(51 82 05 1) ISBN 92-64-12368-7 178 pages   £9.00   US$18.00   F90.00

PROSPECTS FOR SOVIET AGRICULTURAL PRODUCTION AND TRADE (August 1983)
(51 83 06 1) ISBN 92-64-12471-3 118 pages   £6.00   US$12.00   F60.00

PROSPECTS FOR AGRICULTURAL PRODUCTION AND TRADE IN EASTERN EUROPE
Volume I, Poland, German Democratic Republic, Hungary (December 1981)
(51 81 10 1) ISBN 92-64-12262-1 248 pages   £9.50   US$21.00   F95.00

Volume II: Bulgaria, Czechoslovakia, Romania (November 1982)
(51 82 06 1) ISBN 92-64-12369-5 216 pages   £13.00   US$26.00   F130.00

THE INSTABILITY OF AGRICULTURAL COMMODITY MARKETS (February 1980)
(51 80 03 1) ISBN 92-64-12041-6 230 pages   £4.20   US$9.50   F38.00

POSITIVE ADJUSTMENT POLICIES IN THE DAIRY SECTOR (October 1983)
(51 83 09 1) ISBN 92-64-12515-9 96 pages   £5.50   US$11.00   F55.00

OECD FOOD INDUSTRIES IN THE 1980's (November 1983)
(51 83 08 1) ISBN 92-64-12509-4 188 pages   £8.00   US$16.00   F80.00

Prices charged at the OECD Publications Office.

THE OECD CATALOGUE OF PUBLICATIONS and supplements will be sent free of charge
on request addressed either to OECD Publications Office,
2, rue André-Pascal, 75775 PARIS CEDEX 16, or to the OECD Sales Agent in your country.

TABLE OF CONTENTS

Summary 7

Chapter I

TRENDS IN WORLD AGRICULTURAL TRADE 11

- I. Volume of Trade 11
- II. OECD and LDC Shares of World Exports 13
- III. Import Shares 15
- IV. Determinants of Changes in Trade volume and Trade Shares 18
- V. Future Developments in Trade Volume and Trade Shares 20

Chapter II

COMMODITY REVIEW OF OECD-LDC TRADE FLOWS 22

- I. General Trends in Trade Flows 22
- II. Trends in Trade Flows by Commodity Group 27
    - A. Foodgrains and Derived Products 27
    - B. Feedgrains and Substitute Feeds 30
    - C. Oilseeds 34
    - D. Dairy Products 36
    - E. Meat and Poultry 40
    - F. Fruit and Vegetables 42
    - G. Sugar 46
    - H. Tropical Beverages 48
    - I. Agricultural Raw Materials 50
- III. Overview of Commodity Discussion 52

Chapter III

THE EFFECT OF DOMESTIC AND TRADE POLICIES ON OECD-LDC AGRICULTURAL TRADE 57

- I. Perspectives on the Role of Agricultural Trade between OECD and Developing Countries ... 57
- II. Policy Approach to Agriculture and Trade 62
    - A. The OECD Approach to Agriculture and Trade 63
    - B. The LDC Approach to Agriculture and Trade 64
    - C. Overall Effect of OECD and LDC Agricultural Policy Approaches .. 65
- III. Agricultural Trade Policies 67
    - A. National Policies 67
        1. Policies of OECD Countries and their Implications for the Developing Countries 67
            - a) Effects on Developing Country Exporters 67
            - b) Effects on Developing Country Importers 70
        2. The Impact of LDC Policies on OECD Member Countries 72
            - a) The Impact on OECD Exporters 72
            - b) The Impact on OECD Importers 76

B. Multilateral Policies and Actions 78
   1. Food Security 78
      a) Food Aid and Food Finance Programmes 79
      b) Development Assistance 80
   2. Export Earnings Stability 81
      a) International Commodity Agreements and Arrangements 81
      b) IMF: Compensatory Financing Facility 84
      c) EEC: The STABEX Scheme 84
      d) IMF: Buffer Stock Facility 84
      e) The Arab Monetary Fund 85
      f) General Aspects of Export Earnings Stability Schemes 85
   3. Export Expansion 85
      a) The GATT: Its Relationship to the Developing Countries 85
      b) Preferential Trading Arrangements Affecting the Developing Countries . . 87
         i) The Generalised Scheme of Preferences 87
         ii) EEC: Lomé Convention 90
         iii) EEC: Other Special Trading Arrangements 90
         iv) Caribbean Basin Initiative 91
      c) General Problems Related to Preferential Arrangements 91
IV. Non-Agricultural Policies and their Effect on OECD-LDC Agricultural Trade . . . 92
   A. OECD Policies 92
   B. Developing Country Policies 94
   C. Multilateral Policies and Practices 96

Chapter IV

POLICY IMPLICATIONS OF THE DEVELOPMENT OF OECD AGRICULTURAL TRADE WITH DEVELOPING COUNTRIES 98

I. General Implications of the Development of Trade 98
II. National Policies and the Future Development of Trade 100
III. Multilateral Policies and the Future Development of Trade 102
   A. The Multilateral Framework for Rights and Obligations in Trade . . . 102
   B. Measures to Reduce Fluctuations in Commodity Prices and
      the Export Earnings of Developing Countries 103
   C. Food Security 104
IV. Concluding Observations 105

Appendix 106

Notes and references 111

SUMMARY

Agricultural trade has expanded rapidly during the past decade and at the same time has undergone a substantial transformation in its structure. Although intra-OECD trade still accounts for a large proportion of total agricultural trade, the growing demand for agricultural products in the non-OECD countries, driven by rapid income growth in the past 10 years – particularly in the middle-income and OPEC countries – has greatly increased the relative importance of the developing countries as trading partners. As a consequence OECD-LDC agricultural trade issues have become more important and are likely to remain a focal point for discussion throughout the decade. It is, therefore, important to understand how trade between OECD Member countries and the developing countries has evolved over the past decade and what forces have affected its development. Once the trends are identified and the major forces affecting them are understood, it will be possible to obtain a clearer picture of the future structure of agricultural trade and the policy measures which are likely to have the greatest impact on its development throughout the rest of the decade.

This study is a follow-up to the study on *Problems of Agricultural Trade* which was commissioned by the OECD Council at Ministerial Level in June 1979. This report, published in October 1982, focussed on the issues of agricultural trade arising out of trade among OECD countries. The current study broadens the foundation established by its predecessor and develops the analysis of trends and policies pertaining to OECD-LDC agricultural trade.

The first of four chapters identifies the major underlying structural factors affecting the two-way OECD/LDC trade in agricultural commodities. This chapter also examines trade volumes and trade shares on an aggregate basis and highlights the interdependence of the OECD and developing country economies as regards macro-economic policies and the impact of export earnings, terms of trade and income expansion in developing countries on their participation in international markets for agricultural commodities.

Chapter II provides a more detailed analysis of the structural determinants of agricultural trade and trade flows according to commodity and geographical groupings. In addition to providing aggregate trade flow data the major emphasis is on export/import shares, annual growth rates and destination shares broken down by commodity groups and geographical units. Highlights from this chapter include developments such as:

- Rapid population increases in third world countries which have major implications for food-deficit countries; exporting countries and for multilateral initiatives;
- Changing food consumption patterns resulting from rapid urbanisation, and in some developing countries income growth which in turn implies an even greater dependence on imported foodstuffs which are often not produced domestically in adequate quantities;
- The emerging importance of the Newly Industrialised Countries as importers of OECD agricultural commodities – especially feedgrains and protein meals.

These factors have been the primary cause of the increased importance of LDC markets for OECD cereal exports.

Chapter III examines and analyses the effects of domestic and trade policies on the two-way OECD/LDC trade. Major topics include the different approaches to macro-economic, agricultural and trade policies employed by the two groups of countries at respective national levels and multilateral policies and actions which affect OECD/LDC agricultural trade. In addition to published OECD documents this chapter draws upon several trade-oriented studies done by other national or international bodies. The following general points emerge from this Chapter:

- The developing countries should not be viewed as a homogeneous group, but as a collection of diverse countries at different stages of economic development; hence
- Trade liberalisation in all products - not just products currently of interest to the developing countries - is an important aspect of global economic development and both the OECD countries and the LDCs can gain from such policies.
- Market access is an important aspect of economic development and developing countries are encouraged to progressively open their markets to OECD exports in the course of their economic development.
- A variety of multilateral initiatives involving food security, export earnings stability and export expansion highlight the cooperation and interdependence between the OECD countries and the developing countries.

The continued expansion of agricultural trade has important implications for the agricultural sectors of both OECD countries and developing countries. It also has implications for the national and multilateral policies which provide the framework for trade. Chapter IV summarises the general implications of the expansion in trade and the particular implications for policy-makers in OECD member countries. Briefly, Chapter IV stresses the following points:

- The diversity of the developing countries in terms of the nature of their agricultural trade and their economic structure;
- In spite of these diversities, there are numerous shared concerns with respect to agricultural trade;
- The growing interdependence and shared benefits from trade expansion are stressed;
- The issue of the fuller integration of the more advanced developing countries into the multilateral trading system is raised; at the same time, the issue of preferential treatment for the poorer developing countries should also be considered;
- The importance and the operational difficulties of multilateral initiatives to reduce fluctuations in commodity prices and to promote food security are recognised. Better targeting of these measures is suggested in order to improve their effectiveness.

The developing countries have much at stake in the current concern about the health of the international trading system. Due to the great diversity in the stage of development and resource availability of individual developing countries, the benefits which each country may reap from a more open trading system vary widely. Already the pace of development of some economies – notably the NICs – has been stimulated by their more open trading policies. On the other hand, benefits accruing to the poorest LDCs are correspondingly less: these countries may continue to need specific assistance from the OECD countries. Nevertheless it is in the mutual interests of all trading partners – developed or developing – to promote a more open system of agricultural trade.

In spite of occasional strains to the system, on balance, agricultural trade between the OECD area and the developing countries has risen dramatically since the early 1970s and has proved mutually beneficial to both groups of countries. It is evident that continuation of this expansion should be encouraged; however, the growing interdependence between both groups of countries places greater stress on national trade policy-oriented measures and also on the multilateral initiatives which try to promote trade expansion. This web of inter-relationships in both agricultural and non-agricultural trade between the OECD and developing countries requires that considerable caution be exercised by each group in the formulation of national trade-oriented policy measures and in laying the groundwork for multilateral initiatives.

Chapter I

TRENDS IN WORLD AGRICULTURAL TRADE[1]

I. VOLUME OF TRADE

1.1. Table 1.1 gives growth rates for the volume of total world trade (primary commodities plus manufactures), trade in the major agricultural commodities, and world agricultural production over the period 1960-80. It demonstrates that although the average annual rate of growth of trade in agricultural commodities (4.3 per cent) has been lower than that for trade as a whole, (8.2 per cent) it has been relatively high in comparison to the expansion of world agricultural production (2.5 per cent). The volume of agricultural trade increased by over 160 per cent between 1960 and 1980. However, variability in the volume of trade has been considerably higher than for production; averaging 3.1 per cent per annum compared to 0.7 per cent for production[2]. This reflects the residual nature of trade in the world agricultural economy. As an outlet for surpluses, or source of supply in times of shortage, international trade is required to absorb a large part of the natural or policy-induced fluctuations in domestic markets.

Table 1.1

GROWTH AND VARIABILITY IN THE VOLUME OF WORLD TRADE
AND PRODUCTION IN 1960-80

PER CENT

	Average annual rate of growth (1)	Average annual deviation (2)
Agricultural Trade (3)	4.3	3.1
Total World Trade	8.2	2.3
World Agricultural Production	2.5	0.7

1. Compound rates computed from predicted values of trend lines.

2. Average absolute deviation from trend.

3. 1962-1980.

Source: Computed from FAO and U.N. data.

1.2. Table 1.2 presents figures for the rates of growth and variability in the volume of world trade by commodity over the period 1960-1980. Growth rates in the volume of world trade have differed considerably across commodities. At one extreme, the volume of trade in oilseeds and products has expanded at the rapid rate of over 11 per cent per year, while at the other extreme, trade in tropical beverages has only increased by 1.5 per cent per year[3]. Four groups of commodities (oilseeds, feedgrains, meat and dairy products) have demonstrated rates of growth above the average for all commodities. The remainder (foodgrains, fruit, vegetables, sugar, tropical beverages and agricultural raw materials) have had below-average growth rates. It is notable that the high-growth commodities are primarily either direct sources of protein or components of the feed needed to produce such protein.

Table 1.2

RATES OF GROWTH AND VARIABILITY IN THE VOLUME OF WORLD TRADE OF MAJOR AGRICULTURAL COMMODITIES, 1960-1980.

Commodity (1)	Average annual increase (2)	Average annual fluctuation (3)
Meat	6.8	3.6
Dairy Products	5.4	3.4
Foodgrains and products	4.0	7.0
Feedgrains	7.6	5.1
Oilseeds and products	11.3	3.4
Fruit	3.2	2.0
Vegetables	2.7	7.2
Sugar	2.5	3.5
Tropical beverages	1.5	2.7
Agricultural raw materials	3.2	3.4
All above commodities (4)	4.3	3.1

1. Definition of commodity aggregates given in the appendix.
2. Compound growth rate computed from trend values.
3. Average absolute deviation from trend.
4. Computed with respect to the arithmetic mean.

Source: Computed from FAO data.

1.3. In terms of the variability of traded volumes, vegetables and foodgrains have demonstrated the greatest average annual fluctuations, while world trade in fruit has been the most stable. The majority of the commodities with rapid growth in volume have also been relatively stable from year-to-year. Only feedgrains has displayed a rate of variability close to its rate of growth. It has not therefore been the case that the more rapidly growing commodities in world trade have also been the more unstable in terms of volume, in fact if anything the reverse has been the case.

II. OECD AND LDC SHARES OF WORLD EXPORTS

1.4. Recent trends in the OECD's share of world exports for the major commodities and trends in the LDCs share are summarised in Table 1.3[4]. In 1980, the OECD accounted for over 50 per cent of world exports of each of the commodities listed, with the exception of fruit, sugar and tropical beverages[5]. Its share for all commodities was 65 per cent, ranging from a low of 6 per cent for tropical beverages to 95 per cent for dairy products[6]. By comparison, the LDCs accounted for roughly 50 per cent or more of world exports in only three cases, fruit, sugar and tropical beverages. Their share for all the commodities considered was just over 27 per cent.

1.5. Throughout the period analysed, the OECD's export market share of most commodities has tended to increase[7]. In terms of the aggregate volume of all commodities the increase averaged four fifths of 1 per cent of world exports per year, with the largest individual increase being in feedgrains (1.9 per cent per year). For fruits and vegetables there was no trend in the OECD's share of world exports while for oilseeds and products its share declined by an average of 1.5 per cent of world exports per year.

1.6. In contrast to the OECD situation, the LDC's export market share of most commodities has tended to either fall or display no trend. The largest declines have occurred in feedgrains and meat. The sole increase in LDC market share has occurred in oilseeds, which rose at an average rate of 1.7 per cent of world exports per year. This is an important exception, however, since the growth of world trade in this commodity has been particularly rapid (Table 1.2). The LDCs have not managed to maintain their share in the other rapidly growing commodity – feedgrains – at least in part because of increasing domestic requirements.

1.7. The degree of variability in the OECD's export share has differed considerably across products. Its share of vegetable exports was the most unstable with an average annual deviation from trend of 3.4 per cent of world exports. Its share of dairy exports was the most stable with only a 0.5 per cent average deviation. In all cases, the average annual fluctuation in OECD export share exceeded the long-run rate of change in that share, indicating that significant instability exists on the export side of these markets. However, as in the case of total trade, it does not appear that a systematic relationship exists between the rate of change in the OECD's export share and the variability of that share. Specifically, it does not appear that those products in which the OECD's share is changing rapidly are those in which its share is subject to high short-term variability.

1.8. The degree of variability in the LDC's export share has also differed considerably across products. In many cases, the absolute magnitude of this variability has been similar to that of the OECD. However, when the relative magnitude of variability is considered (variability relative to 1980 marketshare) then the variability of LDC export shares is clearly greater for most products than those for the OECD[8]. In terms of market share, therefore, LDC exports of the commodities analysed seem to be more variable than OECD exports[9].

1.9. Table 1.4 provides additional insight into the nature of the change in market share by indicating the relationship (degree of association) between the OECD's share and those of LDCs and Centrally Planned Economies (CPEs). This table indicates those cases in which changes in the OECD's export share have been either strongly or very strongly associated with changes in the shares of other aggregates[10]. For example, the OECD's share of world meat exports has been trending upwards and this increase has been strongly associated with a downward trend in the share of world exports originating from developing countries (LDCs). The OECD's increasing share of world vegetable exports appears to be primarily associated with a declining trend in the share of exports from CPEs. However, the OECD's growing share

Table 1.3

TRENDS IN THE OECD AND LDC SHARES OF WORLD EXPORTS OF MAJOR AGRICULTURAL COMMODITIES 1967-80
Per cent of world exports

	1967 Share of trend		1980 share of trend		Average annual change in share		Average annual fluctuation (1)	
	OECD	LDC	OECD	LDC	OECD	LDC	OECD	LDC
Meat	62.1	22.3 (2)	78.9	10.4	+1.3	-0.9	2.2	2.3
Dairy products	91.0	1.5 (2)	95.4	1.5 (2)	+0.4	0.0	0.5	0.3
Foodgrains and products	68.7	14.4 (2)	79.4	14.4 (2)	+0.9	0.0	2.2	2.7
Feedgrains	63.8	25.1	88.7	6.7	+1.9	-1.4	2.0	2.5
Oilseeds and products	85.4	10.7	67.9	31.5	-1.5	+1.7	2.2	2.2
Fruit	34.7 (2)	49.1 (2)	34.7 (2)	49.1 (2)	0.0	0.0	1.3 (3)	1.1
Vegetables	68.1	12.1 (2)	76.7	12.1 (2)	+0.7	0.0	3.4	1.4
Sugar	14.2	67.3 (2)	27.3	67.3 (2)	+0.5	0.0	1.6	2.5
Tropical beverages	2.1	97.1	5.7	91.7	+0.3	-0.4	0.5	0.6
Agricultural raw materials	64.2	24.4	67.5	20.8	+0.3	-0.3	1.0	0.7
All above commodities	54.3	34.2	65.0	27.3	+0.8	-0.5	0.7	0.6

1. Average absolute deviation from trend.
2. Arithmetic mean.
3. Average deviation from arithmetic mean.

Source: Computed from FAO data.

14

Table 1.4

RELATIONSHIP BETWEEN OECD'S EXPORT SHARES AND THOSE OF OTHER ECONOMIC AGGREGATES 1967-80

Commodity	Trend in OECD share	Negative association (1) Strong	Negative association (1) Very strong	Positive association Strong
Meat	Up	L (2)		
Dairy products	Up		C (3)	
Foodgrains and products	Up			
Feedgrains	Up	C	L	
Oilseeds and products	Down		L	C
Fruit	Stable			
Vegetables	Up		C	
Sugar	Up	C		
Tropical beverages	Up	L		C
Agricultural raw materials	Up	L		
All above commodities	Up		LC	

1. Measure of association = r, the Pearsonian correlation coefficient. Strong association is defined as an absolute value of r greater than 0.80 but less than 0.90. Very strong association is an absolute value of r greater than 0.90.

2. Denotes less -- developed or developing country aggregate.

3. Denotes centrally-planned economies aggregate.

Source: Computed from FAO data.

of world foodgrain exports has not been strongly associated with a systematic loss of market share by any single aggregate, rather it has been more diffuse[11].

1.10. The table indicates that increases in the OECD's export share in two of the agricultural commodities particularly sensitive to the growth in consumer incomes (meat and the feedgrains used to produce animal products) have been associated by declines in LDC export share. The only success story from the LDC point of view has been in oilseeds, in which LDC market share has grown at the expense of OECD share. For agricultural raw materials, a category which includes the traditional export crops of many LDCs, their share has declined as the OECD's share has increased.

III. IMPORT SHARES

1.11. Trends in OECD and LDC shares of world imports of the major agricultural commodities are illustrated by Table 1.5. In 1980, the OECD accounted for 60 per cent of world imports of these commodities. Its share ranged from a low of roughly 20 per cent in the

Table 1.5

TRENDS IN THE OECD AND LDC SHARES OF WORLD IMPORTS OF MAJOR AGRICULTURAL COMMODITIES 1967-80
Per cent of world imports

	1967 Share at trend		1980 share of trend		Average annual change in share		Average annual fluctuation (1)		Relative variability of share	
	OECD	LDC	OECD	LDC	OECD	LDC	OECD	LDC	OECD	LDC
Meat	86.3	5.1	69.1	20.4	-1.3	+1.3	3.1	1.1	.014	.054
Dairy Products	75.2	19.8	57.6	33.5	-1.5	+1.1	2.3	2.0	.040	.060
Foodgrains and products	28.5	50.8 (2)	19.9	50.8(2)	-0.7	0.0	1.6	2.1	.080	.041
Feedgrains	87.8	4.4	47.5	18.2	-3.4	+1.1	2.6	1.3	.055	.071
Oilseeds and products	81.5	9.0	62.3	22.1	-1.6	+1.1	1.4	1.2	.022	.054
Fruit	81.5	9.0	77.3	14.8	-0.7	+0.5	0.6	0.6	.007	.041
Vegetables	63.6 (2)	23.7	63.6 (2)	33.5	0.0	+0.8	2.8 (3)	1.8	.004	.054
Sugar	62.5 (2)	18.6	39.3	30.8	-2.1	+1.0	2.5	2.8	.064	.091
Tropical beverages	83.9	8.4	78.6	11.1	-0.4	+0.2	0.5	0.6	.007	.053
Agricultural raw materials	78.2	10.7 (4)	71.9	14.2	-0.5	+0.3	0.7	0.5	.010	.033
All above commodities	72.6 (4)	15.9 (4)	59.8	22.6	-1.1	+0.6	0.8	0.6	.014	.028

1. Average absolute deviation from trend.
2. Arithmetic mean.
3. Average deviation from arithmetic mean.
4. 1968.

Source: Computed from FAO data.

16

case of foodgrains to a high of 79 per cent in the case of tropical beverages. By contrast, the LDCs accounted for roughly 23 per cent of imports, with the largest share of over 50 per cent being in foodgrains.

1.12. Throughout the period analysed, the OECD's share of world imports of the major commodities has tended to decrease[12]. The sole exception is vegetables where no trend in OECD share is discernible. The rate of decline has been largest (in absolute terms) in the case of feedgrains and sugar, and lowest in the cases of fruit and tropical beverages. For the aggregate of all commodities, the decline in the OECD's market share has averaged 1.1 per cent of world imports per year, a figure which is larger than the increase in its export share (Table 1.3).

1.13. In contrast to the OECD situation, with the exception of foodgrains the LDC's share of imports has tended to increase. The largest absolute increases have occurred in animal products (meat and dairy products) and in the feed necessary to produce these products (feedgrains and oilseeds).

1.14 As in the case of its exports, the degree of variability in the OECD's import shares has differed considerably across products. In absolute terms, the most variable have been meat

Table 1.6

RELATIONSHIP BETWEEN OECD'S IMPORT SHARES AND THOSE OF OTHER ECONOMIC AGGREGATES 1967-80

Commodity	Trend in OECD share	Negative association (1) Strong	Negative association (1) Very strong
Meat	Down	L (2)	
Dairy products	Down		L
Foodgrains and products	Down		
Feedgrains	Down	L	C (3)
Oilseeds and products	Down	C	L
Fruit	Down	C	L
Vegetables	Down		
Sugar	No trend	C	L
Tropical beverages	Down	L	
Agricultural raw materials	Down	C	L
All above commodities	Down		LC

1. Measure of association = r, the Pearsonian correlation coefficient. Strong association is defined as an absolute value of r greater than 0.80 but less than 0.90. Very strong association is an absolute value of r greater than 0.90.

2. Denotes less - developed or developing country aggregate

3. Denotes Centrally Planned Economies aggregate.

Source: Computed from FAO data.

and vegetables while the most stable have been tropical beverages, fruit, and agricultural raw materials. For three products (feedgrains, oilseeds, and fruits) annual variability in OECD market share around trend has been less than its long-run average rate of change. This contrasts with the situation for export shares in which all products had greater short-run variability than their rate of long-term change. Thus there has been greater stability in terms of OECD trade shares for imports than for exports.

1.15. In terms of the variability of the LDC's export shares, the most significant observation is that for all the products considered, with the exception of foodgrains, the *relative* variability of the LDC import share has tended to be greater than that for the OECD import share. As Table 1.6 indicates, for all commodities except foodgrains a falling import share of OECD countries in world trade has been strongly associated with a rising share for the LDCs. Thus, other things being equal, the declining share of the OECD in world imports and the increasing share of the LDCs will have contributed to increased instability in the volume of world imports of most commodities[13].

IV. DETERMINANTS OF CHANGES IN TRADE VOLUME AND TRADE SHARES

1.16. During the past two decades, the volume of world trade in agricultural commodities has increased dramatically. This expansion has been due largely to the rapid growth in world income. Particularly strong growth has occurred in animal products (meat and dairy products) and in the feedgrains and oilseeds used to produce animal products. Consumers in most countries display a marked preference for such products as their incomes rise.

1.17. On the export side of the picture, with the exception of oilseeds and products, the LDC share of world exports of agricultural commodities has tended to stagnate or to decline. To some extent this reflects the supply conditions for the products concerned and the fact that growing domestic demand in many cases has taken precedence over export markets. It also reflects the impact of domestic policies which have depressed the production of agricultural export commodities in LDCs. These factors are discussed more thoroughly in Chapter III.

1.18. Although all exporters face the problem of restricted market access through tariffs and other devices for most agricultural commodities, LDCs have been treated more favourably during the 1970s through the introduction of tariff concessions for example, under the GSP and the Lomé Convention. However, they have also faced increased competition from other suppliers, both those who increasingly oriented their domestic production towards export markets and those who have found it necessary to use world markets as an outlet for surpluses. It is notable that the major LDC export success (oilseeds) has been achieved in a product which is not subject to significant surplus disposal activity and in which market access in principal consuming markets is relatively free. Whether this success will continue would seem to depend largely on whether the accessibility of markets is maintained.

1.19. In terms of the position of LDCs in world agricultural trade, the most striking development in recent years has been their growing share of world imports of all commodities with the exception of foodgrains. This growth has generally been associated with a decline in the share of world imports going to the OECD. The major reasons for this can be inferred from Table 1.7.

1.20. The high population growth rates in both low and middle income LDCs have created a substantial expansion in the potential demand for agricultural products (line 1). Income per

Table 1.7

COMPARATIVE ECONOMIC INDICATORS FOR THE OECD AND LDCs (1)

	OECD	LDCs "Low" income	LDCs "Middle" income
1. Average annual population growth rate, 1970-80 (per cent)	0.7	2.1	2.4
2. Average annual rate of growth in real GDP, 1970-80 (per cent)	3.2	4.6	5.6
3. Average annual rate of growth in exports (all products), 1970-80 (per cent)	5.8	-0.4	3.9
4. Average index of food production per capita 1970-80 (1969-71=100)	111	106	108
5. Debt service as a percentage of goods and services (2)			
in 1970	-	12	16
in 1980	-	17	14
in 1982	-	23	16
6. Food as a percentage of all imports, 1979	12	17	11

1. The rates given are either median values or weighted averages. Country coverage may differ due to the availability of data. See the original source for details and for the criterion used to separate low and middle income LDCs.

2. Data concerning this item are taken from OECD, Development Co-operation 1982 Review, p. 239. Data for 1982 are preliminary.

Source: The World Bank, World Development Report, Washington D.C.

capita (measured by GNP) has been growing at rates in excess of that for the OECD, and has been particularly high in the middle income LDCs (line 2). In those countries in which income per capita has increased, the demand for food has grown rapidly, particularly for the more income elastic foods such as animal products. Furthermore, LDC exports and hence earnings of foreign exchange needed to purchase imports have been growing at a relatively rapid rate in middle income LDCs where the growth in demand for such foods is most rapid (line 3).

1.21. On the production side, the domestic output of food per capita has increased in the LDCs but at a lower rate than in the OECD (line 4). This differential rate of expansion between the two regions has been influenced by technical factors and also by policies (see

Chapter 3). Given the relatively slower rate of growth in per capita demand for food in the OECD as a whole than in LDCs, the expansion of production has meant that the OECD has had food available for sale to countries whose own food demand has been increasing. As a result, the volume of world imports of food and the LDC's share of these imports have both increased rapidly.

1.22. In terms of the stability of world markets, the apparently greater short-run variability of LDC imports than those of the OECD is significant. In the case of meat and, to a lesser extent, dairy products there is evidence that some of this variability is due to normal price responsiveness i.e. when prices rise the LDCs reduce their purchases thus reducing their market share, and vice versa[14]. This does not appear to be the case for feedgrains and oilseeds. Such behaviour can be explained by the fact that LDCs are better able or more willing to change their imports in response to short-term fluctuations in world prices for final consumer products consumed by higher income groups and which are not vital to the maintenance of a basic caloric intake. Adjustment of imports of feedgrains and oilseeds is less feasible either because of the basic importance of the commodities in the diet (e.g. the oil component of oilseeds) or because these commodities are essential inputs into existing livestock production for which rapid adjustment is not possible (feedgrains and the feed component of oilseeds).

1.23. Where LDCs introduce more quantity variability into world markets, if this variability is inversely related to fluctuations in prices then it will contribute to market stability in terms of aggregate revenues and expenditures. Other things being equal, this appears to be the case for meat and possibly dairy products. Where the additional variability does not relate to price then it will tend to destabilize markets. This appears to be the case for feedgrains and oilseeds. A full analysis of the effects of structural change upon variability in world markets would need to examine the implications of changes on the export side, as well as the role of other country groups, particularly the centrally planned economies, in the market. These conclusions can only be considered as a partial assessment of the impact of the growing import shares of the LDCs on the stability of agricultural markets.

V. FUTURE DEVELOPMENTS IN TRADE VOLUME AND TRADE SHARES

1.24. Should existing trends continue, the volume of world trade in agricultural commodities would be roughly 15-20 per cent higher in 1986 than in 1980. The largest increases would occur in animal products and feed (including oilseeds). During the same period, the OECD's share of world imports (including EEC intra-trade) would fall from 60 per cent (at trend) in 1980 to 52 per cent in 1986. LDC import share would rise from 23 per cent in 1980 to 29 per cent in 1986, with the largest increases in shares occurring in animal products and feed[15]. To an increasing extent these trends will depend upon what happens to economic conditions in the LDCs.

1.25. For many LDCs, the increases in world oil prices during the 1970s resulted in severe balance of payments pressures - pressures which have been relieved by international borrowing. In the principal LDC importers of agricultural products, the middle income group, debt service as a percentage of exports has risen significantly (Table 1.7, line 5). In individual countries, ratios considerably in excess of the average have been achieved, in 1981 for example, 32 per cent for Brazil, 45 per cent for Peru, 30 per cent for Morocco and 27 per cent for Bolivia.

1.26. The balance of payments deficits of non-oil producing LDCs rose rapidly between 1978 and the end of 1982, rising from $26 billion to $66 billion, but the 1982 level was below the 1981 high of $78 billion This reflects the sharp increases in oil prices since 1979, the subsequent slowdown of economic activity in industrial countries, the fall in the price of their non-fuel commodity exports in 1981 and in some cases the effect of rising interest costs on outstanding external debt[16]. If the current economic downturn in the LDC's major export markets were to continue for a sustained period time then it would clearly affect the rate of growth in their imports. Their own economic growth rates would be reduced which would lower the demand for imported products. Reduced exports and export earnings would limit their ability to sustain further expansion of international borrowing and to purchase foreign goods.

1.27. Because of the generally lower income elasticities of demand for agricultural products compared to industrial goods, this combination of circumstances would probably have less of an impact upon agricultural than upon industrial imports, particularly since the proportion of total import expenditure devoted to food and agricultural products is not large (Table 1.7, line 6). Nevertheless, a sustained downturn in demand in their major export markets would inevitably affect LDC food imports.

1.28. Economic conditions in the OECD countries are crucial for the future rate of growth in world agricultural imports. Although the OECD's share of world imports has been steadily declining, the direct effect of variations in OECD agricultural imports upon world trade is still significant. A reduction in the rate of growth of GNP in the OECD area would exert a substantial depressing effect upon the rate of increase in world trade. A further indirect effect would be felt through the impact of slow OECD income growth upon the export earnings of other agricultural importers, particularly the middle income LDCs.

1.29. Changes in OECD policies which directly affect the export earnings of LDCs would also have important implications for OECD agricultural exports to those countries. Measures to restrict further the entry of LDC products (both agricultural and non-agricultural) into OECD markets in order to protect domestic industries would limit the purchasing power of LDCs in international markets. This would reduce the rate of expansion in all imports, including agricultural imports. Such relationships highlight the interdependence of the economies of the developing countries and those of the OECD countries.

1.30. In LDCs themselves, particularly those in which import expansion has been greatest, a reduction in incomes and foreign exchange earnings could generate pressures to expand domestic agricultural output in order to maintain domestic employment and to save foreign exchange. Import substitution is not easy to achieve in the short-run due to agriculture's inherent structural rigidity, but in the longer-term some substitution of domestic for imported products may be feasible. This would affect the rate of growth of world trade in these products and the rate of increase of the LDC's share of such trade. In the short-term, the rate of growth of trade could be strongly affected if LDCs were forced to reduce their imports of more income elastic "luxury" agricultural goods such as animal products and feeds in order to deal with depressed earnings of foreign exchange.

1.31. All the factors outlined above could exert downward pressure on LDC demand for OECD agricultural exports and hence upon the prices of these exports. Whether this pressure will actually occur depends largely on the future rate of economic growth in the OECD area. The supply of exports does not appear to be a limiting factor, at least in the medium term, although volumes will be influenced by changes in agricultural and trade policies in exporting countries and by weather conditions. The key issue in terms of supply is whether the volume of OECD agricultural exports will adjust in line with changes in the determinants of demand. If the rate of growth in demand for agricultural imports by LDCs declines, the price-depressing effect of this decline will be amplified if domestic support programmes in exporting countries, and in particular in the OECD area, prevent necessary adjustment in world supply.

Chapter II

COMMODITY REVIEW OF OECD-LDC TRADE FLOWS

I. GENERAL TRENDS IN AGRICULTURAL TRADE FLOWS

2.1. As indicated in Chapter I the volume of world trade in agricultural products has grown at a more rapid rate than world agricultural production but, has not kept pace with total world trade. A more comprehensive picture of the growth of agricultural exports relative to total trade is shown in Table 2.1 which presents OECD and LDC agricultural trade, as a per cent of merchandise trade, to various destinations for 1972, 1975 and 1980[17]. A notable change is the

Table 2.1

AGRICULTURAL EXPORTS AS A PER CENT OF TOTAL EXPORTS TO VARIOUS DESTINATIONS, 1972, 1975, 1979, 1980

Destination	OECD Exports			LDC exports		
	1972	1975	1980	1972	1975	1979
OECD and Yugoslavia	11.5	11.1	9.1	23.7	14.1	13.1
EEC	17.9	16.1	11.0	24.9	14.8	16.1
EFTA	7.6	7.4	5.9	27.8	17.7	16.0
Other Western Europe	9.1	9.0	10.1	25.2	17.3	14.2
United States	8.3	7.3	6.0	27.5	14.9	10.6
Canada	7.5	7.1	6.6	14.8	7.9	10.8
Japan	23.1	27.0	24.3	12.5	10.1	8.6
Australia and New Zealand	5.1	4.3	4.3	12.3	9.8	9.9
CPEs	17.6	13.0	20.6	39.4	48.6	75.5
LDC	11.9	11.8	12.2	21.1	15.3	13.0
Africa	12.8	13.1	15.4	29.1	25.5	22.0
Latin America	10.3	9.8	12.7	15.0	9.9	10.7
Western Asia	11.5	8.6	11.8	32.6	29.9	18.6
Eastern Asia	12.8	15.0	9.3	20.5	12.3	11.2
Oceania	22.8	27.5	25.2	15.0	6.5	8.7
World	11.8	11.4	10.8	23.2	15.6	14.1

Sources: OECD Statistics of Foreign Trade, Series C.

UNCTAD Handbook of International Trade and Development Statistics, 1981 Supplement.

Table 2.2

INDICES OF OECD AGRICULTURAL EXPORTS TO VARIOUS DESTINATIONS, ADJUSTED FOR CHANGES IN UNIT VALUES (1), 1972-1980

	1972	1973	1974	1975	1976	1977	1978	1979	1980
OECD and Yugoslavia	100.0	104.7	92.3	89.3	104.7	106.5	113.6	119.4	118.9
CPEs	100.0	114.1	74.6	106.6	148.7	109.5	135.4	189.8	214.5
LDCs	100.0	112.0	131.4	140.6	139.8	154.8	182.1	192.7	241.4
Africa	100.0	108.2	137.2	158.5	155.2	188.5	209.7	216.1	283.8
North	100.0	118.0	171.7	198.9	171.0	198.4	217.3	246.0	317.2
Southern	100.0	98.0	101.4	116.8	138.9	178.2	201.8	185.1	249.4
Latin America	100.0	112.2	130.9	112.6	112.0	121.7	150.1	155.2	225.8
Western Asia	100.0	107.2	165.4	189.0	214.4	275.1	319.3	356.2	439.7
Eastern Asia	100.0	119.5	120.1	142.0	131.0	121.2	146.9	157.0	162.5
Oceania	100.0	79.5	78.1	74.9	93.0	98.8	113.7	116.2	121.6
OPEC	100.0	102.9	148.7	182.5	194.2	258.5	268.8	301.0	398.0
NICs	100.0	161.4	165.4	148.4	143.8	157.4	215.4	235.0	314.5
Poorest LDCs	100.0	103.7	121.9	120.0	130.3	144.9	161.5	165.4	202.5
World	100.0	108.0	102.0	103.5	116.4	118.9	132.6	144.0	158.5

1. An agricultural unit value index for developed countries (1969-71 = 100) from the FAO Trade Yearbook was used to adjust the original undeflated value data.

Source: OECD Statistics of Foreign Trade, Series C.

Table 2.3

INDICES OF LDC AGRICULTURAL EXPORTS TO VARIOUS DESTINATIONS ADJUSTED FOR CHANGES IN UNIT VALUES (1), 1972-1980.

	1972	1973	1974	1975	1976	1977	1978	1979
OECD and Yugoslavia	100.0	101.3	88.9	87.2	102.8	101.8	82.5	111.8
EEC	100.0	101.1	85.3	80.9	97.6	102.6	71.5	112.7
EFTA	100.0	104.1	85.2	84.6	114.8	106.4	76.6	101.9
Other W. Europe	100.0	116.4	111.0	131.7	130.6	122.1	110.0	130.5
United States	100.0	91.8	79.6	75.0	94.5	89.8	81.9	95.4
Canada	100.0	82.2	107.7	81.7	81.0	71.4	79.9	96.2
Japan	100.0	133.5	124.3	144.0	145.0	134.3	130.5	161.8
Australia and New Zealand	100.0	95.9	148.3	120.2	120.4	110.7	133.8	154.8
CPEs	100.0	114.3	118.1	175.3	174.1	169.2	170.7	182.3
LDCs	100.0	101.7	113.9	126.3	120.1	115.7	127.8	156.1
Africa	100.0	110.8	140.4	156.6	144.8	137.1	129.1	139.7
Latin America	100.0	95.9	91.7	133.7	119.3	110.6	127.9	187.3
Western Asia	100.0	103.8	179.7	187.6	163.3	147.5	169.7	191.4
Eastern Asia	100.0	100.8	89.4	87.1	95.0	99.0	110.7	133.0
Oceania	100.0	75.3	105.3	79.3	50.9	19.6	122.7	89.1
OPEC	100.0	144.4	37.0	247.5	240.5	236.6	224.5	274.7
World	100.0	103.4	98.9	102.1	112.8	110.7	116.3	127.8

1. An agricultural unit value index for developed countries (1969-71 = 100) from the FAO Trade Yearbook was used to adjust the original undeflated value data.

Source: UNCTAD, Handbook of International Trade and Development Statistics, 1976 and Supplement 1980.

sharp decline in the agricultural proportion of LDC exports to all destinations since 1972, which has also prompted a sharp increase in the proportion of LDC imports. The volume of agricultural exports (Table 2.3) by LDCs to OECD countries remained almost stable, while the index of OECD agricultural exports to the developing countries increased rapidly (Table 2.2). In fact, in 1981 these trends seem to have become even more marked, although sufficient data concerning 1981 were not available for extensive analysis. Table 2.1 also illustrates the important differences among different destinations. For OECD exports, the regions taking the highest proportionate share of agricultural goods are Japan, the Centrally Planned Economies (CPEs), Africa and Oceania. Overall the LDCs have a higher proportion of agricultural products in their exports relative to OECD countries, thus they have a greater dependence on agricultural exports for earning foreign exchange[18]. Agricultural trade accounts for almost half of all LDC trade destined for the CPE countries and more than 20 per cent of LDC exports to Africa and West Asia.

2.2. An indication of the growth of agricultural exports by the OECD and LDCs to various destinations is given in Tables 2.2 and 2.3. OECD agricultural exports to all destinations, after adjustments for changes in unit values, increased by 58.4 per cent between 1972 and 1980. The increase in intra-OECD trade was below this (35.4 per cent increase) while exports to the CPE and developing countries increased by a much larger amount (114.5 and 141.5 per cent respectively). Among the LDCs, Africa and West Asia showed the greatest increase. Certain countries in the first two regions experienced rapid growth in per capita incomes as a result of petroleum price increases and responded by purchasing more agricultural products.

2.3. The increase in LDC agricultural exports – (shown in Table 2.3) – has been much less than the growth in OECD exports (27.8 per cent increase for LDCs in 1979 versus a 49.4 per cent increase for OECD). This is largely the result of two factors:

1. Slower growth in export availabilities in many LDCs, relative to OECD countries, due to increasing demands on agricultural output from domestic consumption; and

2. A mix of agricultural exports which has been characterised by slower worldwide growth in import demand relative to that of products exported by OECD countries (i.e. the worldwide demand for sugar, tropical beverages, rubber and cotton, for example, has increased much more slowly than the worldwide demand for foodgrains, feedgrains, oilseeds and livestock products).

2.4. The main growth markets for LDC agricultural exports, with the exception of Japan and Australia/New Zealand, have been the other LDCs (i.e. South-South trade) and CPE countries. LDC agricultural exports to the OECD declined in relative importance during the 1970s since they, at best, remained constant while exports to other destinations increased. The only market in which LDC exports clearly increased more rapidly than those of the OECD is the CPE category.

2.5. The changing structure of OECD/LDC commodity trade is shown in Table 2.4[19]. The major OECD exports to LDCs are grains, dairy products/eggs and meats which accounted for 40 per cent, 12 per cent and 8 per cent, respectively of total shipments in 1980. Major OECD imports from LDCs are tropical beverages and vegetables/fruits which amounted to 39 per cent and 16 per cent respectively in 1980. The data also indicate changes in percentage shares over time, notable examples are: an increase of OECD exports to LDCs of feedgrains and products (11.7 per cent in 1980 versus 5.8 per cent of total in 1972); the declining share of OECD meat and poultry imports from LDCs (10.1 per cent of total in 1972 versus 3.8 per cent in 1980); and, the increasing share of OECD tropical beverages (31.1 per cent of total in 1972

Table 2.4

CHANGES IN THE STRUCTURE OF OECD AGRICULTURAL TRADE
Per cent

Commodity Groups (1)	OECD Exports to All Destinations		OECD Exports to LDCs		OECD Imports from All Sources		OECD Imports from LDCs	
	1972	1980	1972	1980	1972	1980	1972	1980
Agricultural trade	100.0	100.0	100.0	100.0	100.0	100.0	100.0	100.0
Foodgrains and products	16.8	19.2	34.4	28.6	4.1	4.4	0.5	0.5
Feedgrains and products	10.8	15.8	5.8	11.7	8.0	10.1	6.3	4.1
Oilseeds and products	12.2	12.2	4.8	5.5	12.3	14.1	9.8	9.7
Meats and poultry	12.9	9.6	6.2	8.1	15.7	9.1	10.1	3.8
Dairy and eggs	7.2	6.7	14.0	11.6	2.8	1.9	0.2	0.0
Vegetables and fruits	11.2	10.0	5.5	5.8	17.0	17.8	17.1	16.5
Tropical beverages	1.9	2.0	1.1	1.1	13.7	18.0	31.1	39.0
Sugar and Honey	3.4	5.0	4.5	6.7	7.2	6.4	12.2	10.0

1. See Appendix Table A.3 for a definition of commodity groupings. Percentages do not sum to 100 because not all components are represented.

Source: OECD Statistics of Foreign Trade, Series C.

26

versus 39.0 per cent in 1980). The share of each commodity group, as a percentage of total agricultural trade, should be borne in mind when considering the more detailed analyses of commodity trade flows which follow.

2.6. The following sections provide a more detailed commodity analysis of the broad categories included in Chapter I. Emphasis will be on identifying trends in OECD/LDC trade flows and on determining the factors responsible for the direction and (where relevant) the changes in those trends.

II. TRENDS IN TRADE FLOWS BY COMMODITY GROUP

A. Foodgrains and Derived Products

2.7. OECD countries are major exporters of foodgrains to developing countries, hence this section focuses on the role of developing countries as markets for OECD foodgrain exports. Table 2.5 shows the major OECD exporters of foodgrains and products and the proportion of their exports going to different markets in 1972 and 1980. The bottom row shows the total value of all foodgrains and products exported in million current U.S. dollars. There has been a sharp drop in the export share of foodgrains and derived products for intra-OECD markets, declining from 27.8 per cent to 17.4 per cent in nine years. If intra-EEC trade in foodgrains and derived products is included, intra-OECD trade amounted to 23.2 per cent of total trade in 1980 compared with 30.0 per cent in 1972, due to the fact that OECD import requirements have expanded more slowly than the import requirements of other markets.

2.8. The CPEs and almost all of the LDC groupings have become relatively more important importers of OECD foodgrains as increasing population, rising incomes, changing tastes and preferences and lagging agricultural productivity have made it necessary to increase foodgrain imports. The only developing country region where the proportion of total OECD foodgrain exports has not increased is East Asia. This is primarily due to increased domestic output in India (which lowered import requirements) and increased maize and rice output in Thailand (which, although an exporter is included in this regional grouping).

2.9. The foodgrain import demand from the LDCs is due to varied factors such as continued pressures from population growth, decreasing domestic output per capita (especially in the poorest LDCs) and the rapid income growth in OPEC countries where the proportion of total OECD foodgrain exports has increased from 10.3 to 16.5 per cent (Table 2.5). Such factors are responsible for the large share increases which have occurred in North Africa, West Asia and sub-Saharan Africa where most of these countries are located. The proportion of exports from the EEC and Canada to LDCs has increased sharply while the share of total Australian exports to LDCs has declined; the proportion of U.S. exports to LDCs has not changed. The pattern emerging is one of exporter concentration in nearby LDC regions with the EEC increasing its share to Africa, Canada increasing its share to Latin America, and Australia increasing its share to West Asia as the proportion of its exports to other LDC regions declines. The U.S. has made the largest adjustment to the decline in Indian foodgrain import demand as a large proportion of U.S. exports previously destined for East Asia have been shifted to other LDC regions.

2.10. The average annual growth rate of OECD exports of foodgrains and products, after correcting for changes in unit values, was 6.9 per cent per year between 1972 and 1980 (Table 2.6). Australia had the highest growth rate among the four OECD exporters (15.6 per cent per annum) as a result of rapid expansion in sales to Centrally Planned and West Asian

Table 2.5

FOODGRAINS AND DERIVED PRODUCTS -- EXPORT SHARES
Per cent

	OECD and Yugoslavia 1972	OECD and Yugoslavia 1980	EEC 1972	EEC 1980	Canada 1972	Canada 1980	United States 1972	United States 1980	Australia/New Zealand 1972	Australia/New Zealand 1980
OECD and Yugoslavia	27.8	17.4	25.8	12.9	31.2	23.6	23.4	28.6	33.3	9.2
CPEs	15.3	17.1	12.8	18.5	25.6	31.2	12.9	7.0	9.3	27.3
LDCs	49.1	54.3	59.8	66.8	20.4	32.4	59.6	59.3	57.2	50.3
Africa	11.0	18.8	34.8	44.6	4.7	7.2	5.8	13.9	18.8	13.4
North	7.0	12.6	17.6	30.9	3.3	6.2	3.6	7.4	15.1	12.2
Southern	4.2	6.1	17.3	13.6	1.4	1.0	2.2	6.5	3.7	1.1
Latin America	11.3	12.7	6.8	4.5	9.1	18.2	15.2	19.2	8.7	0.5
Western Asia	4.8	9.4	6.5	12.1	1.4	4.2	5.1	7.1	7.7	18.7
Eastern Asia	21.2	12.9	11.0	5.5	5.2	2.7	33.5	19.1	17.6	14.2
Oceania	0.7	0.6	0.5	0.2	0.0	0.0	0.1	0.1	4.3	3.6
OPEC	10.3	16.5	8.7	21.0	3.8	9.4	14.5	15.6	7.1	20.4
NICs	9.0	10.4	2.5	1.5	2.7	11.0	15.7	16.4	4.7	4.0
Poorest LDCs	13.2	14.7	31.9	23.7	3.6	2.9	9.6	13.4	23.0	21.9
World	100.0	100.0	100.0	100.0	100.0	100.0	100.0	100.0	100.0	100.0
In $ million	(4 200.2)	(18 241.1)	(553.6)	(3 534.8)	(1 015.1)	(3 536.4)	(1 966.8)	(7 804.8)	(508.3)	(2 485.6)

Note: The value of intra-EEC exports amounted to $836 million in 1972 and $3 165.4 million in 1980.

Source: OECD Statistics of Foreign Trade, Series C.

28

Table 2.6

OECD EXPORTS OF FOODGRAINS AND DERIVED PRODUCTS
AVERAGE ANNUAL GROWTH, 1972-1980 (1)
Per cent

	OECD	EEC	USA	Canada	Australia/New Zealand
OECD and Yugoslavia	0.0	2.5	3.5	0.0	1.2
CPEs	24.2	41.9	25.4	53.7	72.6
LDCs	8.4	15.8	7.7	11.4	16.4
Africa	13.9	18.3	20.4	27.2	25.2
North	15.8	29.0	19.0	41.9	30.6
Southern	13.1	9.6	26.5	2.2	3.3
Latin America	10.8	7.4	15.2	22.0	29.7
Western Asia	17.7	20.6	15.6	63.5	40.3
Eastern Asia	2.7	16.5	3.0	5.8	14.7
Oceania	2.8	-2.8	8.0	23.0	5.6
OPEC	13.5	27.3	7.2	49.5	40.3
NICs	14.7	9.7	14.5	85.6	7.7
Poorest LDCs	7.6	9.0	12.4	5.7	26.6
World	6.9	12.9	8.3	4.0	15.6

1. Corrected for changes in unit values.

Source: <u>OECD Statistics of Foreign Trade, Series C.</u>

countries. The U.S., EEC and Canada had annual growth rates averaging 8.3, 12.9 and 4.0 per cent, respectively. Growth in CPE and LDC markets was more important to all exporters than growth in OECD markets. The poorest LDC markets – where the potential but not the effective foodgrain demand is the greatest – had growth rates above the world average but their share of the market and their rate of import growth remarried well below that of the wealthier LDCs, NICs and OPEC.

2.11. The volume and the trade shares of international grains markets have also been affected by policy measures such as food aid, bilateral agreements and export assistance. Food aid has played a very important role in grain shipments in the past 30 years although the relative importance of these shipments has declined in the 1970s. The last decade has also witnessed an increase in the use of institutional arrangements – both national and international – to channel food aid to developing countries. One of the most significant has been the establishment of the World Food Program which has been designed to monitor and provide co-ordination of national food aid programmes, as well as vehicle of multilateral food aid. Bilateral agreements accounted for as much as 40 per cent of world trade in grains in 1982[20]. Although these may affect the trade shares of certain countries, they probably have very little effect on the size of the market. Export assistance in its various forms has had significant impacts on the volume and trade shares of the international market for food grains and derived products.

B. Feedgrains and Substitute Feeds

2.12. Over the period studied, feedgrains were one of the fastest growing commodity categories in agricultural trade. As noted in Chapter I, higher consumer incomes have led to a growing demand for livestock products and meat – products in which feedgrains are a major input. A number of items are included in this category but (see explanatory Appendix Table A.3) maize, barley and other unmilled coarse grains accounted for 77 per cent of OECD exports and 62 per cent of OECD imports in 1980. Mixed feeds, hay fodder, cassava, meat and fish meals and bran account for the remainder.

2.13. The U.S. is the dominant OECD exporter of feedgrains and related products, accounting for almost 60 per cent of the OECD exports in this group in 1980. Table 2.7 shows the export destination shares of the U.S. as well as total OECD exports of feedgrains and related products. Export shares for the years 1972, 1979 and 1980 are also included, because the U.S. suspension of grain sales to the USSR in 1980 distorted trade flows.

2.14. The destination shares in Table 2.7 indicate a shift away from OECD markets towards CPE and LDC markets, although the shift has not been as dramatic as was evident for foodgrains. All LDC geographic regions have increased in relative importance – with the exception of those countries in Oceania and Southern Africa. The economic breakdown of LDCs, however, provides additional information. The NICs and OPEC – the two groups of LDCs where income growth has been the greatest – have both greatly increased their relative shares of OECD feedgrain exports while the poorest LDCs have experienced only a slight increase, if any, in the proportion of OECD feedgrain and related product exports which they represent. The ability of the NICs and OPEC countries to further expand purchases will depend to a large extent on their international financial situation. For example, Brazil and Mexico, among the NICs, and Nigeria (an OPEC member) are facing serious financial difficulties due to huge foreign debts and slackening world demand for their exports. The situation for Taiwan and South Korea is less serious since they have smaller international debts and broader-based export sub-sectors. The OPEC members, of course, depend on strong relative petroleum prices for their growing volume of trade.

Table 2.7

DESTINATION SHARES OF OECD AND US EXPORTS OF FEEDGRAINS AND SUBSTITUTE PRODUCTS
1972, 1979, 1980
Per cent

	OECD 1972	OECD 1979	OECD 1980	UNITED STATES 1972	UNITED STATES 1979	UNITED STATES 1980
OECD and Yugoslavia	64.9	49.6	49.3	68.2	49.8	52.7
CPEs	19.6	25.5	19.0	15.0	25.8	14.9
LDCs	12.8	20.9	28.9	13.3	19.9	29.0
Africa	1.6	3.2	4.5	1.0	1.7	3.1
North	1.0	2.6	3.1	0.5	1.3	1.9
Southern	0.5	0.6	1.4	0.5	0.4	1.2
Latin America	5.4	7.3	14.3	7.4	8.9	17.8
Western Asia	1.2	2.8	3.6	0.8	1.4	1.1
Eastern Asia	4.3	7.4	6.4	4.0	7.9	7.0
Oceania	0.3	0.1	0.1	0.0	0.0	0.0
OPEC	2.0	4.4	5.8	1.5	2.1	2.4
NICs	3.7	11.2	15.2	4.4	13.7	19.3
Poorest LDCs	1.6	1.4	2.8	1.8	1.2	3.0
World	100.0	100.0	100.0	100.0	100.0	100.0
In $ million	(2 706.9)	(10 856.5)	(14 104.4)	(1 696.6)	(8 222.6)	(10 475.1)

Note: The value of intra-EEC exports amounted to $1 086.4 million in 1972 and $3 858.8 million in 1980.

Source: OECD Statistics of Foreign Trade, Series C.

Table 2.8

SOURCE SHARES OF OECD, EEC AND JAPANESE IMPORTS OF FEEDGRAINS AND SUBSTITUTE PRODUCTS 1972, 1979, 1980
Per cent

	OECD 1972	OECD 1979	OECD 1980	EEC 1972	EEC 1979	EEC 1980	Japan 1972	Japan 1979	Japan 1980
OECD and Yugoslavia	62.8	70.0	78.4	58.4	58.4	61.6	69.5	77.3	88.9
CPEs	1.0	0.9	0.8	1.1	1.1	1.1	0.4	0.3	0.2
LDCs	28.3	26.3	16.8	33.5	38.1	32.6	17.5	16.9	5.2
Africa	3.4	1.1	0.9	3.6	1.7	1.9	2.3	0.8	0.0
North	0.7	0.2	0.4	1.2	0.3	0.8	0.1	0.0	0.0
Southern	2.6	0.9	0.5	2.3	1.4	1.1	2.3	0.8	0.0
Latin America	19.1	15.0	6.7	23.0	16.3	11.2	6.9	13.0	3.1
Western Asia	0.2	0.0	0.0	0.1	0.0	0.0	0.7	0.0	0.0
Eastern Asia	5.5	10.1	9.0	6.9	20.1	19.4	7.5	3.1	2.0
Oceania	0.0	0.0	0.0	1.3	0.0	0.0	0.0	0.0	0.0
OPEC	1.6	2.1	1.7	2.5	4.1	3.2	1.1	0.8	0.9
NICs	11.9	12.0	4.0	15.3	12.5	7.8	6.5	11.6	1.5
Poorest LDCs	3.8	2.5	1.8	4.2	4.5	3.7	3.0	1.2	0.5
World	100.0	100.0	100.0	100.0	100.0	100.0	100.0	100.0	100.0
In $ million	(3 031.2)	(9 300.2)	(10 499.5)	(1 555.2)	(4 168.7)	(4 464.0)	(784.3)	(2 813.0)	(3 447.1)

Note: The value of intra-EEC exports amounted to $1 110.0 million in 1972 and $3 521.9 million in 1980.

Source: OECD Statistics of Foreign Trade, Series C.

2.15. Imports of feedgrains and related products by OECD countries since 1972 are coming increasingly from OECD sources (principally the U.S.) as shown in Table 2.8. The major LDC exporting regions for these commodities are Latin America and East Asia dominated by Argentina and Thailand, respectively. Latin America's proportion of OECD imports had fallen slightly by 1979 but fell very sharply in 1980 as Argentine exports were diverted to the Soviet Union after the U.S. sales suspension.

2.16. The import shares for the two largest OECD markets for feedgrains and related products (the EEC and Japan) reflect differences in the development of trade. Japan greatly increased its imports of feedgrains and related products, particularly from the United States. This is reflected by the increase in share of imports derived from the OECD area. The major development in EEC shares has been the increase in the proportion of imports obtained from East Asia, reflecting the rapid rise in imports of cassava from Thailand. Recently the EEC has negotiated voluntary restraint agreements with both Thailand, Brazil and Indonesia on this product. Imports of other cereals substitutes e.g. corn gluten feed by the EEC have also been increasing due to favourable price relationships and the absence of import restrictions[21].

2.17. The average 1972-1980 growth rates in Table 2.9 emphasize the changes which occurred in the trade of feedgrains and related products between the OECD and developing countries. OECD exports to all destinations grew at an annual average rate of 10.4 per cent while exports to LDCs and CPEs grew at rates of 23.0 and 26.5 per cent respectively. In contrast, imports of feedgrains and related products by OECD countries increased at a rate of

Table 2.9

AVERAGE GROWTH RATES OF OECD. TRADE IN FEEDGRAINS AND SUBSTITUTE PRODUCTS, 1972 to 1980 (1)
Per cent

	Imports			Exports	
	OECD	EEC	Japan	OECD	USA
OECD and Yugoslavia	7.8	5.0	11.6	6.7	9.5
CPEs	5.2	7.3	4.4	26.5	34.8
LDCs	0.0	2.7	0.4	23.0	26.8
Africa	-10.5	-2.8	-1.4	28.5	38.3
North	5.5	11.2	-10.4	28.5	42.8
Southern	-11.4	-2.5	0.9	37.2	47.8
Latin America	-3.3	-4.8	11.0	30.2	33.4
Western Asia	-14.6	27.0	-35.6	26.0	20.7
Eastern Asia	12.2	17.4	-2.9	17.8	28.3
Oceania	34.6	-11.8	-20.2	0.2	16.0
OPEC	9.4	10.2	250.7	25.9	23.7
NICs	-1.2	-3.4	6.7	35.9	41.9
Poorest LDCs	-1.0	6.7	-3.3	26.8	32.2
World	4.4	2.9	7.5	10.4	3.1

1. Corrected for changes in unit values.

Source: OECD Statistics of Foreign Trade, Series C.

only 4.0 per cent per year with OECD purchases from LDCs and from within the OECD increasing at roughly the same rate. EEC imports from developing countries grew at a faster rate than its imports from OECD countries but most of this growth was due to rising cassava imports from Thailand. Japan's purchases from the NICs (among which Argentina is the largest feedgrain exporter) showed strong growth. Overall, however, these figures indicate that, with the possible exceptions of Thailand and Argentina, the developing countries are becoming less important as sources of OECD imports of feedgrains and products. On the other hand, LDCs are becoming increasingly important markets for OECD feedgrain exports.

C. Oilseeds and Products

2.18. The crushing of oilseeds yields the joint products – meal and oil – each destined for different end uses. Protein meals from soyabeans, peanuts, cottonseeds, sunflower seeds, copra, rapeseed and palm kernels are all used as animal feeds. Vegetable oils from the same products are used primarily in the food industry and for certain industrial products. The demand for protein meals has become the driving force behind the growth in world trade of oilseeds within which soyabeans are the most important, accounting for about 75 per cent of world trade in protein meals. The primary exporter of soyabeans is the U.S. followed by Brazil and Argentina – both of which have greatly expanded production in response to strong world demand. The major importers of OECD oilseeds and meals have been Western Europe, Japan

Table 2.10

DESTINATION SHARES OF OECD EXPORTS OF OILSEEDS AND PRODUCTS, 1972 AND 1980

Per cent

	OECD 1972	OECD 1980	United States 1972	United States 1980
OECD and Yugoslavia	81.8	74.9	84.9	77.0
CPEs	6.0	5.4	4.9	5.3
LDCs	7.9	13.4	8.3	15.0
Africa	0.9	1.8	0.0	0.3
Latin America	2.3	5.6	3.0	8.0
Western Asia	0.7	1.0	0.4	0.4
Eastern Asia	3.7	4.9	4.8	6.2
Oceania	0.2	0.1	0.0	0.0
OPEC	1.4	3.1	0.8	2.2
NICs	1.4	7.5	1.6	10.4
World	100.0	100.0	100.0	100.0
In $ million	(3 043.2)	(11 636.0)	(2 249.1)	(9 261.4)

Note: The value of intra-EEC exports amounted to $624 million in 1972 and $2 569 million in 1980.

Source: OECD Statistics of Foreign Trade, Series C.

Table 2.11

SOURCE SHARES OF OECD, EEC AND JAPANESE IMPORTS OF OILSEEDS
AND PRODUCTS, 1972 and 1980
Per cent

	OECD 1972	OECD 1980	EEC 1972	EEC 1980	Japan 1972	Japan 1980
OECD and Yugoslavia	63.7	67.9	58.0	61.9	79.3	83.1
USA	48.5	55.7	46.8	56.2	62.4	64.2
CPEs	1.1	0.8	1.4	0.7	0.4	0.4
LDCs	31.7	29.0	37.8	35.3	13.3	11.7
Africa	8.6	2.8	10.5	3.5	4.0	1.0
North	2.5	10.0	3.3	1.2	1.5	0.3
Southern	6.0	1.8	7.2	2.3	2.5	0.7
Latin America	15.9	20.9	19.4	25.2	1.7	6.6
Western Asia	0.3	0.2	0.3	0.2	0.7	0.0
Eastern Asia	6.6	4.7	7.4	5.9	6.6	2.8
Oceania	0.3	0.7	0.3	0.6	0.4	1.3
OPEC	3.1	2.0	4.1	2.6	2.5	1.5
NICs	9.9	17.9	13.6	22.4	0.8	3.9
Poorest LDCs	11.0	4.7	13.0	5.8	5.8	2.2
World	100.0	100.0	100.0	100.0	100.0	100.0
In $ million	(4 214.5)	(14 601.1)	(2 508.5)	(9 207.4)	(790.1)	(2 466.4)

Note: The value of intra-EEC exports amounted to $663.1 million in 1972 and $2 609.1 million in 1980.

Source: OECD Statistics of Foreign Trade, Series C.

and Eastern Europe. Developing countries have become more significant importers in the past decade and account for 13.4 per cent of OECD exports (Table 2.10) of which the seven NICs of East Asia and Latin America account for 7.5 per cent. U.S. oilseed and meal exports have shifted towards the LDCs away from the CPE countries, while exports to the EEC have stabilised.

2.19. More than two-thirds of OECD imports of oilseeds and meals came from OECD sources during the study period with most of the rest coming from developing countries (Table 2.11). Latin America was the largest LDC supplier and its share increased from 15.9 to 20.9 per cent: the U.S. was the predominant OECD supplier with a share that increased from 48.5 to 55.7 per cent over the period. In the OECD's two largest import markets for oilseeds and meals, the EEC and Japan, both the U.S. and Latin America increased their market shares. This probably reflects the ability of both of these regions to expand production to meet the growing demand as well as a preference by importers for soyabeans produced by these regions (partly due to a price advantage over alternative oilseeds).

2.20. Japan relies primarily on the U.S. for its oilseeds but also imports 10-15 per cent of its requirements from LDCs – primarily from Latin America and East Asia. In recent years the purchases from East Asia have fallen while imports from Latin America have risen.

2.21. Oilseed imports by OECD countries have grown at an average annual rate of 5.8 per

Table 2.12

AVERAGE GROWTH RATES OF OECD OILSEED TRADE WITH SELECTED MARKETS, 1972-1980 (1)
Per cent

	Imports	Exports
OECD and Yugoslavia	6.8	6.4
United States	7.9	1.7
CPEs	5.3	17.5
LDCs	5.3	15.3
Africa	-7.2	19.8
North	0.5	20.7
Southern	-7.8	22.2
Latin America	9.9	28.0
Western Asia	-20.6	14.1
Eastern Asia	4.0	13.8
Oceania	34.1	-1.9
OPEC	3.7	21.6
NICs	15.8	43.7
Poorest LDCs	-4.0	17.7
World	5.8	7.8

1. Corrected for changes in unit values.

Source: OECD Statistics of Foreign Trade, Series C.

cent over the 1972-1980 period (Table 2.12). Of the two main sources – the U.S. and Latin America – the latter has shown the most rapid growth (9.9 per cent per annum). In fact, Latin American exports might have grown even faster had it not been for Brazilian policies favouring export of soyabean products rather than the raw beans.

2.22. During the study period, exports of oilseeds and meal from OECD countries expanded rapidly to almost all developing country markets – an average annual rate of 15.3 per cent, compared with a rate of 6.4 per cent annually for intra-OECD exports. Data for OPEC and the NICs show that it is largely these two groups of countries within the LDCs which are the driving force behind this growth in import demand. Yet even the poorest countries had an annual average growth of almost 18 per cent.

D. Dairy Products and Eggs

2.23. The OECD countries are by far the largest suppliers of dairy produce entering world trade and over half of OECD exports consist of intra-EEC trade. Only small quantities (about 5 per cent of their total imports[22] in 1980) are imported by OECD countries from LDC and/or CPE regions. This section is thus confined to a discussion of the role of developing countries in OECD export trade in dairy produce.

Table 2.13

DESTINATION SHARES OF OECD EXPORTS OF DAIRY PRODUCTS AND EGGS, 1972 AND 1980
Per cent

	OECD 1972	OECD 1980	EEC 1972	EEC 1980	Australia/New Zealand 1972	Australia/New Zealand 1980	United States 1972	United States 1980
OECD and Yugoslavia	47.1	27.7	32.4	17.3	58.0	37.0	29.9	21.9
CPEs	4.5	7.4	4.2	8.1	0.6	5.2	8.1	0.0
LDCs	46.8	65.7	61.0	73.0	40.6	57.1	60.8	76.9
Africa	13.0	19.8	27.7	26.8	1.7	1.9	5.4	5.8
North	6.6	10.1	14.6	13.3	0.1	0.1	2.0	1.0
Southern	6.4	9.7	13.0	13.5	1.7	1.8	3.4	4.8
Latin America	15.4	16.1	16.3	17.5	13.0	10.5	39.2	50.9
Western Asia	5.2	16.3	8.7	20.5	2.9	20.5	1.6	11.6
Eastern Asia	12.2	10.9	8.0	8.0	21.0	31.4	14.3	7.8
Oceania	0.9	0.6	0.4	0.1	2.0	3.0	0.3	0.8
OPEC	10.6	25.1	20.0	30.3	4.2	17.5	4.8	12.7
NICs	5.7	7.6	3.6	5.9	3.8	9.1	23.4	37.9
Poorest LDCs	9.7	13.3	14.6	15.7	7.7	13.5	8.5	8.8
World	100.0	100.0	100.0	100.0	100.0	100.0	100.0	100.0
In $ million	(1 792.6)	(6 336.9)	(744.4)	(4 131.7)	(566.0)	(1 037.8)	(143.4)	(235.0)

Note: The value of intra-EEC exports amounted to $1 491.0 million in 1972 and $6 525.9 million in 1980.

Source: OECD Statistics of Foreign Trade, Series C.

2.24. Table 2.13 presents data for trade in dairy and eggs (SITC 02); eggs, however, accounted for only about 6-7 per cent of total trade over the period. Most of this trade was intra-EEC and to a lesser extent imports by LDCs.

2.25. Trade trends in dairy products are about the same as for OECD exports of grains and oilseeds i.e. a rise in the relative share of exports to developing countries and a fall in intra-OECD exports. This is a process which has been under way for a lengthy period and by 1972 the share of developing countries in OECD exports had already risen to 47 per cent: by 1980 it had reached 64 per cent. The increase in the relative importance of the developing countries reflects the relative stability in overall demand for imports by OECD countries[23] and an increase in that by developing countries.

2.26. In many OECD countries milk production has been rising faster than domestic demand in recent years. Reasons for this imbalance are varied (according to individual countries); however, general reasons such as declining per capita consumption, increased output per animal due to technical factors, attractive cost/price relationships for producers, etc. could be cited. Sluggish domestic consumption has resulted in a large increase in export availabilities in the OECD region as a whole, and in some parts a decline in imports.

2.27. This has particularly been the case for the EEC, traditionally a heavy importer from Australia/New Zealand but whose purchases from these countries fell sharply during 1972-80. Australia and New Zealand have therefore been forced to develop other markets, as far as possible within the OECD area but in practice to a greater extent outside. Until 1979 developing countries were the only alternative. In 1979 the USSR began to import dairy products on a significant scale, but at first only relatively small quantities were imported from Australia/New Zealand and in 1980 developing countries took 57 per cent of these countries' dairy exports compared with 37 per cent by OECD countries and only 6 per cent by the USSR and Eastern Europe. In 1972 only 41 per cent of their exports went to developing countries. Geographically, these exports are concentrated in the East Asian area (55 per cent of exports to LDCs in 1980), reflecting the efforts made by these two exporters to encourage the development of re-combining plants[24]. West Asia took 20 per cent of total exports in 1980 and Latin America took about 11 per cent; this represented a relative decline in the importance of Latin America since 1972.

2.28. The EEC strengthened its position as a dairy exporter during the period, mainly because of a sharp expansion in its exports to developing countries. These increased from 61.0 per cent of total EEC exports (including intra-trade) in 1972 to 73.0 per cent in 1980. Food aid accounted for about 25 per cent of exports of the volume of skim milk powder and 9 per cent of exports of butter to developing countries in 1980. Although Africa remained the principal destination, taking over one-third of all exports to developing countries, West Asia and to a lesser extent Latin America grew in importance over the period.

2.29. In spite of cyclical swings in its dairy exports, exports of dairy products by the U.S. were erratic during the period under study, but have risen substantially in recent years. A large proportion of these exports are made on concessional terms to developing countries. Though smaller than in 1970 and 1971, exports were higher in 1972 than in the rest of the period under review; there had been some scarcity of supplies on the world market at the beginning of the decade and the United States had been able to supply butter to Europe and relatively large quantities of skim milk powder to developing countries. The latter remained the principal outlet for U.S. dairy exports, taking 77 per cent of the total in 1980 compared to 61 per cent in 1972. Mexico was the largest single destination.

2.30. The increase in the share of OECD exports going to LDCs has been accompanied by some changes in the geographical distribution of trade. Though African developing countries are the largest destination and have grown somewhat in relative importance over the period

Table 2.14

OECD EXPORTS OF DAIRY PRODUCTS AND EGGS. AVERAGE GROWTH RATES, 1972-1980 (1)

Per cent

OECD and Yugoslavia	1.1
CPEs	34.4
LDCs	12.3
Africa	13.3
North	13.9
Southern	13.1
Latin America	11.9
Western Asia	24.3
Eastern Asia	6.3
Oceania	1.9
OPEC	20.1
NICs	18.5
Poorest LDCs	12.6
World	8.2

1. Corrected for changes in unit values.

Source: OECD Statistics of Foreign Trade, Series C.

the fastest increase has been in exports to West Asia, which took one-quarter of all exports to developing countries in 1980 and whose purchases from OECD grew at an average annual rate of 24.3 per cent between 1972 and 1980 (see Table 2.14). The importance of rising incomes is shown by the large increase in the share of OPEC countries, from 10.6 to 25.1 per cent of all OECD exports and a growth rate of 20.1 per cent; in addition they accounted for 39 per cent of all exports to developing countries in 1980. The NICs increased their share only slightly, while the share of the poorest LDCs rose from 5.7 to 7.6 per cent of total exports, a partial reflection of the role of food aid.

2.31. As regards individual dairy products exported to developing countries, exports of cheese more than trebled over the period, as did those of butter and butter-oil. Exports of milk powder roughly doubled; it is probable that within this group of products exports of skim milk powder expanded at a faster rate than those of whole milk powder.

2.32. The role of the LDCs in world dairy trade is recognised in the International Dairy Arrangement (IDA), which was one of the results of the MTN. The IDA encompasses whole and skim milk powder, milk fat and certain cheeses and aims "to expand and liberalise world trade in dairy products; to achieve greater stability in world trade; to avoid surpluses, shortages, undue price fluctuations, and (more generally) serious disturbances in world trade; and to improve international co-operation in these areas"[25]. The IDA contains provisions for setting minimum export prices, data collection procedures and other "orderly marketing" guidelines. Several provisions pertain specifically to developing countries which promote trade in these products between these regions and dairy exporting countries.

E. Meat and Poultry

2.33. The international meat trade[26] has undergone profound changes in the last decade. Historically, beef has been the most important part of the international meat trade and this part was and still is dominated by trade flows between Oceania and North America. Also during the last 10 years, cyclical production patterns and counter-cyclical beef import quotas in North America have had a clear impact on production and trade by Australia and New Zealand. However, during the 1970s a series of other factors gradually became more important in the international meat market: the emergence of the EEC as an important exporter of beef; the rapidly increasing share of poultry in international meat trade; an increasing number of countries participating in meat export trade; the rapid expansion of markets outside the OECD, particularly in the OPEC region; a series of prolonged economic recessions in OECD countries which has depressed meat demand in major OECD importing countries, while shifting the demand to relatively cheaper meats, e.g. pigmeat and poultry. These developments have altered trade flows, and have increased the competition in international trade between countries and between meats. In 1980 almost 10 per cent of OECD's exports of meats and livestock was poultrymeat, almost as much as the share held by

Table 2.15

SOURCE AND DESTINATION SHARES OF OECD TRADE WITH LDCs IN MEAT AND POULTRY EXPORTS AS A PER CENT OF TOTAL -- 1972 AND 1980
Per cent

	Imports		Exports	
	1972	1980	1972	1980
OECD and Yugoslavia	53.7	65.6	85.5	60.0
CPEs	16.6	14.1	1.4	8.2
LDCs	27.4	17.4	12.5	30.7
Africa	1.3	0.6	1.6	7.3
North	0.1	0.1	0.7	5.3
Southern	1.2	0.5	0.9	2.0
Latin America	25.4	15.4	5.2	5.5
Western Asia	0.0	0.0	2.2	13.2
Eastern Asia	0.7	1.5	2.0	3.3
Oceania	0.0	0.0	1.4	1.3
OPEC	0.1	0.1	1.7	14.4
NICs	20.9	12.8	2.4	3.6
Poorest LDCs	1.2	1.1	1.5	5.1
World	100.0	100.0	100.0	100.0
In $ million	(5 035.1)	(9 405.3)	(2 983.3)	(9 114.0)

Note: The value of intra-EEC exports amounted to $3 402.8 million in 1972 and $11 350.8 million in 1980 and the value of intra-EEC imports amounted to $3 404.5 million in 1972 and 11 390.2 million in 1980.

Source: OECD Statistics of Foreign Trade, Series C.

sheepmeat (11.3 per cent). In 1972 these shares were 3.8 and 12.8 per cent respectively. The share of bovine meat has remained relatively stable at around 35 per cent. The increasing importance of LDC markets for OECD exports of meat (note increases in LDC shares in Table 2.15) reflects to a large extent growing exports of poultrymeat to these destinations. About 5 per cent of the OECD poultrymeat output is now being exported, and about two-thirds of these shipments go to the LDCs and NICs, with the latter markets becoming increasingly important. During the past decade the volume of OECD exports of poultrymeat to the LDCs and NICs climbed steadily, almost quadrupling, while exports to CPE countries fluctuated with no discernible trend. The major exporters of poultrymeat to these destinations are the U.S., the EEC and Brazil. Exports of beef and particularly sheepmeat and live sheep to OPEC and CPE countries have also risen, although with substantial fluctuation in the case of the USSR. The sheepmeat trade and the trade in live sheep to these destinations is dominated by Australia and New Zealand. For sheepmeat meat these traditional exporters have encountered increasing competition from the EEC.

2.34. OECD meat imports from developing countries (Table 2.15) have risen in recent years, partially as a result of preferential trade arrangements such as the Lomé Convention. This does not appear to have affected the distribution of OECD import shares since all LDC exporting regions except East Asia have declined in importance since 1972.

Table 2.16

OECD TRADE IN MEATS AND POULTRY. AVERAGE GROWTH RATES, 1972-1980 (1)
Per cent

	Imports	Exports
OECD and Yugoslavia	2.1	1.5
CPEs	-3.1	74.6
LDCs	-3.6	18.3
Africa	-6.9	31.3
North	3.6	43.8
Southern	-7.5	18.4
Latin America	-3.9	6.2
Western Asia	110.5	36.3
Eastern Asia	16.2	13.0
Oceania	69.6	4.7
OPEC	11.9	40.4
NICs	-2.3	11.8
Poorest LDCs	-1.4	29.6
World	-0.5	5.3

1. Corrected for changes in unit values.

Source: OECD Statistics of Foreign Trade, Series C.

2.35. The average annual growth rates (adjusted for changes in unit value) reflect the changing structure in meat trade (Table 2.16). OECD exports of meat and poultry have increased at a rate of 5.3 per cent annually since 1972. Exports to LDC destinations, however, have expanded much more rapidly (18.3 per cent). Latin America (6.2 per cent) and Oceania (4.7 per cent) were the only LDC regions to which OECD exports increased at rates below the average. OECD imports of meat and poultry have grown more slowly than exports and the growth has come primarily from within the OECD and, in particular, within the EEC. High growth rates for the LDC regions of West Asia (110.5 per cent), East Asia (16.2 per cent) and Oceania (69.6 per cent) have resulted because of their small relative importance as OECD suppliers.

2.36. Trade in meat both intra-OECD and between the OECD and other regions faces a complex array of regulations and policies which affect trade flows. The most notable measures are the import restrictions applied by most OECD countries (e.g. Canada, EEC, Japan, U.S.) which have a major influence on trade flows of beef of OECD exporters such as Australia, New Zealand and Yugoslavia, particularly when diminishing opportunities in the OECD markets have coincided with the emergence of new markets, especially in the NICs and OPEC countries. Such restrictions also affect meat exports of some non-OECD exporters in Latin America. The introduction in October 1980 of a Sheepmeat Regime in the EEC has not yet had a discernible impact on trade.

2.37. Animal health standards and sanitary regulations also have a significant impact on trade flows. Most OECD and Central American countries as well as Korea forbid imports of animals and of uncooked meat from countries where major animal diseases are endemic. This severely limits the number of meat exporters which can gain access to these markets.

2.38. The Arrangement regarding Bovine Meat, under the auspices of the GATT, is a recent multilateral instrument which seeks to promote the expansion, liberalisation and stability of the international meat and livestock markets by facilitating the lowering of trade barriers, and encouraging co-operation among exporters and importers. An additional objective is to improve the opportunities of developing countries to expand their trade in meat and live animals. This Arrangement is of a purely consultative nature and lacks economic provisions, nevertheless it is a step in the right direction toward (a) multilateral cooperation in the meat trade and (b) recognising, and attempting to overcome some of the problems confronting importers/exporters (particularly the LDCs) in international markets[27].

F. Fruit and Vegetables

2.39. This category is the most heterogenous group of commodities/products considered in the study. Tables 2.17 and 2.18 contain supporting data, in value terms, which is highly aggregated and therefore does not provide breakdowns such as citrus/non-citrus fruits, fresh fruit/dried fruit, whether the fruits or vegetables are fresh or semi-processed etc. However, it is evident that the fruits and vegetables group is one of the few where developing countries have maintained their share of an expanding OECD market. Table 2.17 provides a comparison of the percentage distribtuion by origin of OECD fruit and vegetable imports for 1972 with 1980. The proportion of imports from developing countries has remained relatively constant over the study period at around 40 per cent. East Asia and the NICs increased their export shares between 1972 and 1980, the share from the poorest LDCs remained constant, while shares from the other non-OECD regions declined.

2.40. OECD exports of fruits and vegetables to OECD destinations have declined as a share of total exports while the share of exports going to LDCs has increased. The increases to LDC

Table 2.17

SOURCE AND DESTINATION SHARES OF OECD TRADE WITH LDCs
IN FRUIT AND VEGETABLES, 1972 and 1980
Per cent

	Imports 1972	Imports 1980	Exports 1972	Exports 1980
OECD and Yugoslavia	45.4	45.8	81.6	70.6
CPEs	3.9	2.6	6.0	7.5
LDCs	40.1	41.3	11.7	21.2
Africa	8.8	6.5	2.6	4.4
North	5.5	3.8	1.2	2.8
Southern	3.2	2.7	1.3	1.6
Latin America	19.9	19.4	5.0	7.4
Western Asia	1.7	1.4	1.0	4.7
Eastern Asia	9.6	13.9	2.6	4.4
Oceania	0.1	0.0	0.5	0.4
OPEC	4.7	2.6	2.4	6.3
NICs	10.3	12.2	4.0	7.4
Poorest LDCs	8.3	8.6	1.7	2.6
World	100.0	100.0	100.0	100.0
In $ million	(5 832.0)	(17 342.8)	(2 801.3)	(9 496.9)

Note: The value of intra-EEC exports amounted to $1 865.2 million in 1972 and $6 220.0 million in 1980 and the value of intra-EEC imports amounted to $1 885.7 million in 1972 and $6 132.3 million in 1980.

Source: OECD Statistics of Foreign Trade, Series C.

destinations are spread over all regions. Yet in 1980, 70.6 per cent of all OECD fruit and vegetable exports were still to OECD destinations.

2.41. OECD imports of fruits and vegetables increased at an average annual rate of 10.0 per cent between 1972 and 1980 after adjusting for changes in unit values (Table 2.18). The growth rate for developing countries exports to OECD was 10.0 per cent and the least developed group's exports to the OECD grew at an annual rate of 10.1 per cent. These rates may overstate the case, however, as the single year growth rates for 1979-80 for most developing countries were negative.

2.42. Income growth in LDCs is unlikely to play a very important role in the expansion of future trade in fresh fruit and vegetables, particularly in OECD exports. This is due to the perishable nature of the produce which requires the availability of suitable equipment for handling and storage and to the consumer preferences in these countries. However, an expansion is likely to occur as regards trade in dried or processed fruit and vegetables is likely to expand since the same constraints do not apply.

Table 2.18

AVERAGE GROWTH RATES FOR OECD TRADE IN VEGETABLES AND
FRUITS, 1972-1980 (1)
Per cent

	Imports	Exports
OECD and Yugoslavia	10.0	9.6
CPEs	4.8	15.5
LDCs	10.1	20.1
Africa	6.0	19.6
North	5.7	24.6
Southern	7.8	14.8
Latin America	9.4	18.7
Western Asia	11.9	37.1
Eastern Asia	15.1	19.9
Oceania	-2.8	7.1
OPEC	3.1	26.2
NICs	13.0	22.2
Poorest LDCs	10.1	19.5
World	9.7	11.5

1. Corrected for changes in unit values.

Source: OECD Statistics of Foreign Trade, Series C.

2.43. The OECD markets are already well supplied with fresh tropical fruits. In the near future, it is not expected that these supplies will be substantially increased, except perhaps for certain particularly exotic fruits which have special consumer appeal, although within certain limits so as to maintain prices at a profitable level.

2.44. As regards fresh vegetables, the situation differs considerably from that prevailing for fruit. The marketing, in OECD countries, of off-season vegetables mostly from LDCs could certainly increase provided the suitable technical conditions required for their transport to the consuming centres are fulfilled.

2.45. In order to increase LDC exports of processed fruits and vegetables, it will be necessary to create and maintain a necessary industrial infrastructure which would ensure the quality of the produce.

2.46. While the standardisation of fresh and dried fruit as well as fresh vegetables, as recommended by the UN/ECE and implemented by the OECD scheme, may be at first considered as a possible hindrance to the development in exports of these products, it must be recognised that, in the absence of standardisation, it would be impossible to have any organised international trade in this sector.

2.47. In view of the perishable nature of fresh fruit and vegetables and the packaging and transport costs to the large consuming centres, it is obvious that only high quality produce is

Table 2.19

SOURCE SHARES OF OECD IMPORTS OF SUGAR 1972-80
Per cent

OECD Imports from:	1972	1973	1974	1975	1976	1977	1978	1979	1980
OECD and Yugoslavia	23.5	23.3	18.1	17.9	27.0	27.2	30.3	24.3	25.0
CPEs	1.8	3.0	2.7	1.4	1.2	1.1	1.2	1.4	0.9
LDCs	67.9	67.0	82.1	74.5	65.1	64.4	62.7	67.9	65.4
Africa	7.9	7.7	21.6	7.1	8.9	10.9	13.3	14.2	12.2
North	0.3	0.3	0.7	0.1	0.2	0.2	0.5	0.7	0.3
Southern	7.7	7.4	6.2	7.1	8.7	10.7	12.8	13.5	12.0
Latin America	44.0	44.2	50.6	47.0	36.4	35.1	34.6	39.1	38.5
Western Asia	0.1	0.2	0.1	0.0	0.0	0.1	0.1	0.1	0.2
Eastern Asia	11.8	13.4	15.3	18.5	18.5	15.7	11.8	11.0	11.5
Oceania	3.1	1.6	1.0	1.9	1.2	2.5	3.0	3.5	2.9
OPEC	1.6	1.4	0.9	0.4	0.5	0.4	0.4	1.0	1.0
NICs	13.4	16.7	21.6	14.8	9.9	12.7	11.6	14.3	14.0
Poorest LDCs	11.3	12.7	12.3	12.2	9.6	11.5	8.2	8.5	10.7
World	100.0	100.0	100.0	100.0	100.0	100.0	100.0	100.0	100.0

Note: The value of intra-EEC exports amounted to $357.7 million in 1972 and $1 074.4 million in 1980.

Source: OECD Statistics of Foreign Trade, Series C.

likely to ensure remunerative prices. When the produce is transported by air, the costs do not allow marketing at prices which do not take account of this factor. When maritime transport is used, its duration implies the strict application of rules to preserve quality and the use, for certain products, of post-harvest preserving agents which are authorised by the importing countries so as to ensure that the consignments reach the consuming centres in good condition.

2.48. As regards processed (juices, canned products) or dried fruit and vegetables, the efforts currently made by FAO/WHO Codex Alimentarius to set up minimum quality criteria should facilitate trade. Member countries should be encouraged to apply the recommended standards so as to reduce the difficulties arising from the application of regulations which are quite different from one country to another.

G. Sugar

2.49. Agricultural and trade policies affecting sugar have been the focus of growing international tension in recent years. Major OECD sugar consuming countries support and protect their domestic sugar producers and the associated trade restrictions and policy measures have had major effects on trade shares and trade flows. Such measures have had a significant impact on both developed and developing country sugar exporters.

2.50. During the period under review there was little change in the proportion of OECD sugar imports from OECD and LDC sources (Table 2.19). There was, however, a realignment of export shares among developing countries in which Africa gained at the expense of Latin America and East Asia.

2.51. Within individual OECD import markets, there were some major shifts, some of which can be attributed to policy changes (see Table 2.20). In 1976 EEC purchases shifted somewhat from Latin America to African suppliers, as a result of the signing of the Lomé Convention (see para. 3.116) which gave tariff preferences to ACP countries. In addition to being a major sugar importer, the EEC is also an important exporter: its proportion of net exports has risen over the past decade.

2.52. The U.S., a major sugar importer, sharply increased the proportion of its purchases from Latin America in 1979 while the proportion from East Asia fell, reflecting a change in the sugar import policy which shifted from a quota system to a system of largely unrestricted sugar imports.

2.53. This change enabled Latin American exporters to take advantage of lower transportation costs which could not be fully exploited under a quota system. In 1982 the U.S. reimposed sugar quotas and levies as a part of its domestic sugar policy. Special consideration was given to Caribbean sugar exporters in determining quota levels: in general, these quotas reflect the historical performance of these countries in the U.S. market. Since these quotas are a recent development, it is not clear what effect they will have on trade flows. Domestic sugar prices which are supported above the world price level will, however, allow major sugar substitutes – particularly high fructose corn syrup – to remain competitive with cane and beet sugar (in the absence of substantial increases in domestic maize prices) and gain a larger share of the U.S. sweetener market.

2.54. The negative average annual growth in OECD sugar imports (-3.0 per cent) and the 7.6 per cent growth in OECD sugar exports have heightened export problems for LDCs (see Table 2.21), especially during the recent prolonged period of falling prices. This evolution reflects the fact that during the period under study the trading position of the OECD area shifted from net importer to net exporter status. This shift has prompted several countries to

Table 2.20

SOURCE SHARES OF EEC, U.S. AND JAPANESE IMPORTS OF SUGAR 1972-1980
Per cent

	1972	1973	1974	1975	1976	1977	1978	1979	1980
EEC -- Imports from									
LDCs	76.0	80.9	82.1	89.0	86.7	88.6	86.7	86.5	88.8
Africa	25.6	23.3	21.6	24.2	35.5	38.0	39.7	37.1	41.4
Latin America	44.3	53.2	54.4	51.7	41.5	38.5	36.5	35.5	36.1
World	100.0	100.0	100.0	100.0	100.0	100.0	100.0	100.0	100.0
USA -- Imports from									
LDCs	88.9	88.1	89.1	81.4	82.7	78.4	78.9	82.1	82.3
Latin America	61.2	57.4	63.5	58.1	56.8	53.0	56.7	68.6	65.1
Eastern Asia	26.0	28.0	23.4	20.7	24.1	21.7	19.5	5.6	9.3
World	100.0	100.0	100.0	100.0	100.0	100.0	100.0	100.0	100.0
Japan -- Imports from									
OECD	24.2	27.6	13.3	11.8	41.1	40.1	49.1	40.4	33.7
LDC Total	11.2	14.7	25.8	43.1	37.3	34.0	24.0	34.3	32.2
Latin America	40.0	37.8	43.5	32.8	8.9	9.5	12.0	10.6	10.5
Eastern Asia	11.2	14.7	25.8	43.1	37.3	34.0	24.0	34.3	32.2
World	100.0	100.0	100.0	100.0	100.0	100.0	100.0	100.0	100.0

Source: OECD Statistics of Foreign Trade, Series C.

Table 2.21

AVERAGE ANNUAL GROWTH RATES OF OECD SUGAR TRADE BY
SOURCE AND DESTINATION, 1972-1980 (1)
Per cent

	Imports	Exports
OECD and Yugoslavia	-1.7	-1.7
CPEs	-6.2	69.3
LDCs	-2.8	16.2
Africa	3.1	9.4
North	40.4	9.2
Southern	3.1	12.1
Latin America	-3.2	39.9
Western Asia	178.2	37.5
Eastern Asia	-3.5	19.9
Oceania	7.5	2.6
OPEC	7.9	23.9
NICs	2.7	31.0
Poorest LDCs	-1.2	5.4
World	-3.0	+7.6

1. Corrected for changes in unit values.

Source: OECD Statistics of Foreign Trade, Series C.

initiate procedures under Article XXIII of the GATT concerning in particular the export policies of the EEC. However these countries have suspended this procedure pending developments in respect of the renegotiation of a new International Sugar Agreement. In a separate action Nicaragua initiated procedures under Article XXIII in early 1983 concerning reductions in the United States' import quota for sugar from Nicaragua.

2.55. The failure of the International Sugar Agreement to achieve its target price objectives, increased world production and the subsequent build-up of world stocks have caused problems for many sugar exporting countries, in particular those developing countries where sugar exports are an important source of foreign exchange earnings. A decreased demand for sugar in developed countries and competition from substitutes (maize sweeteners) in certain markets could also affect a recovery in prices. As a consequence there is a likelihood of persisting oversupply during the next few years with consequent downward pressure on prices. Such a market situation could have adverse consequences for those LDCs which are heavily dependent on sugar exports.

H. Tropical Beverages

2.56. Tropical beverages – including coffee, tea and cocoa are almost exclusively developing country agricultural products. Africa south of the Sahara and Latin America are the two main sources of supply with shares of 29.6 and 50.7 per cent respectively of the OECD market in

Table 2.22

SOURCE SHARES OF OECD IMPORTS OF COFFEE, TEA AND COCOA,
1972 AND 1980
Per cent

	1972	1980
OECD and Yugoslavia	8.5	8.0
CPEs	0.3	0.2
LDCs	90.8	91.1
Africa	32.4	29.6
North	0.1	0.1
Southern	32.3	29.6
Latin America	48.5	50.7
Western Asia	0.1	0.0
Eastern Asia	9.5	9.2
Oceania	0.3	1.5
OPEC	7.4	8.9
NICs	27.2	22.1
Poorest LDCs	33.7	33.4
World	100.0	100.0
In $ million	(4 691.2)	(18 642.1)

Note: The value of intra-EEC exports amounted to $382.7 million in 1972 and $2 239.8 million in 1980.

Source: OECD Statistics of Foreign Trade, Series C.

1980. In aggregate these shares and the shares of other exporting regions have changed very little over the past decade (Table 2.22) although there may have been significant changes in individual commodities.

2.57. In addition, the OECD market for tropical beverages has grown slowly due primarily to market saturation (Table 2.23). The average annual growth rate in the value of imports (after adjusting for inflation) was only 1.5 per cent for the 1972-1980 period. Developing countries which rely heavily on these commodities to earn foreign exchange face a stagnant market and declining terms of trade. The fact that production from such tree crops is a long-term undertaking hampers the response to changing market conditions, thus promoting structural surpluses.

2.58. Separate attempts have been made in all three commodities to manage world markets, particularly for production and quantities marketed, and have met with varying degrees of success. (See paragraphs 3.92 – 3.96 and Table 3.12). Inherent price instability has been a constant problem and recently depressed economic conditions in major consuming countries (OECD) have dampened demand. A prolonged period of generally low commodity prices has added to the above problems. The existing cocoa agreement has had problems due to a variety of reasons: for example, Ivory Coast – a major producer – remains outside the agreement as does the U.S. – a major consumer. The agreement has also had problems with the level of its

Table 2.23

AVERAGE GROWTH RATES FOR OECD IMPORTS OF COFFEE, TEA,
COCOA AND SPICES, 1972-1980 (1)
Per cent

OECD and Yugoslavia	1.4
CPEs	-3.3
LDCs	1.0
Africa	-0.2
North	-1.0
Southern	-0.1
Latin America	1.8
Western Asia	-8.3
Eastern Asia	0.8
Oceania	54.7
OPEC	4.1
NICs	-0.9
Poorest LDCs	0.8
World	1.0

1. Corrected for changes in unit values.

Source: OECD Statistics of Foreign Trade, Series C.

intervention price and stocks have accumulated. The coffee agreement has been somewhat more successful by using export quotas; nevertheless, stocks have accumulated as demand has decreased. Arrangements for tea have been in effect at various times since the 1930s but a formal agreement has not been established.

I. Agricultural Raw Materials

2.59. The commodities in the agricultural raw materials category are also a very heterogeneous group. In 1980, OECD imports of the major products in this category could be broken down as follows: textile fibres, 20.9 per cent; pulp and waste paper, 17.3 per cent; cork and wood, 42.9 per cent; rubber, 10.5 per cent, and hides and skins 8.3 per cent. Among these products, textile fibres and hides and skins have declined in relative importance since 1972 while the other three sub-groups (pulp and wastepaper, cork and wood and rubber) have increased as a proportion of total group OECD imports.

2.60. Developing countries in many areas of the world rely heavily on the foreign exchange earnings of products in the agricultural raw materials group. OECD countries purchased 24.6 per cent of all their agricultural raw material imports from developing countries in 1980 (Table 2.24). It is significant that, of this, nearly 10 per cent came from the least developed countries. These countries often rely on only one or two major exports to maintain their economies and to provide foreign exchange. They are therefore heavily dependent on the economic well-being and activity of their major export destinations. Agricultural raw materials are more sensitive to fluctuations in the business cycles of partner trading countries than are exports of food products, since these products are inputs into manufacturing and construction which are more sensitive to recession than other sectors of the economy. Exports of these products provide a tenuous foundation for economic development. Nevertheless, many developing country exporters of such products have made progress in diversifying their export base to include less recession-prone commodities.

Table 2.24

SOURCE AND DESTINATION SHARES OF OECD AGRICULTURAL RAW MATERIAL TRADE WITH LDCs, 1972 AND 1980
Per cent

OECD:

	Imports 1972	Imports 1980	Exports 1972	Exports 1980
OECD and Yugoslavia	60.6	60.3	80.8	72.4
CPEs	7.5	7.6	5.8	5.1
LDCs	27.7	28.1	11.5	17.2
Africa	7.5	6.0	1.5	2.9
North	1.9	1.5	1.0	2.3
Southern	5.5	4.5	0.5	0.6
Latin America	6.0	4.8	2.9	3.4
Western Asia	1.0	0.5	1.1	2.1
Eastern Asia	13.2	16.7	5.8	8.7
Oceania	0.7	0.2	0.1	0.0
OPEC	4.1	5.6	1.9	3.8
NICs	5.0	4.2	4.7	7.8
Poorest LDCs	10.6	11.1	2.0	2.5
World	100.0	100.0	100.0	100.0
In $ million	(16 140.6)	(50 467.5)	(11 064.3)	(37 045.8)

Note: The value of intra-EEC exports amounted to $2 401.5 million in 1972 and $7 380.0 million in 1980 and the value of intra-EEC imports amounted to $2 296.7 million in 1972 and 7 298.5 million in 1980.

Source: OECD Statistics of Foreign Trade, Series C.

2.61. OECD exports of agricultural raw materials are primarily destined for OECD markets but the proportion purchased by developing countries is gradually increasing. East Asia had the biggest increase in share. This reflects growing cotton exports (U.S., Turkey) to the NICs (Taiwan, Hong Kong, South Korea) which have become major producers and exporters of textiles and clothing. Future cotton exports to these countries will depend on

Table 2.25

AVERAGE PERCENTAGE GROWTH IN OECD AGRICULTURAL
RAW MATERIAL TRADE, 1972-1980 (1)
Per Cent

	Imports	Exports
OECD and Yugoslavia	4.2	4.0
CPEs	4.2	3.4
LDCs	5.9	10.0
Africa	2.1	14.4
North	4.6	17.5
Southern	1.9	7.1
Latin America	1.3	7.8
Western Asia	2.4	13.8
Eastern Asia	10.6	10.7
Oceania	34.3	-2.4
OPEC	12.6	15.0
NICs	2.8	11.8
Poorest LDCs	7.3	8.1
World	4.5	5.1

1. Corrected for changes in unit values.

Source: OECD Statistics of Foreign Trade, Series C.

economic conditions and import policies in OECD markets. Trade in textiles is currently regulated under the Multi-Fibre Arrangement of the GATT (see para. 3.152).

2.62. OECD imports of agricultural raw materials grew at an average annual rate of 4.5 per cent – only slightly slower than OECD exports at 4.9 per cent (Table 2.25). Developing countries, on average, had higher rates of trade growth than did the OECD aggregate.

III. OVERVIEW OF COMMODITY DISCUSSION

2.63. This chapter has examined the broad trends in agricultural trade flows between OECD countries and the less developed countries for nine commodity groupings. Key determinants of agricultural trade, which were first noted in Chapter I, have again emerged in the more detailed discussions in this chapter. Regional differences in the income elasticity of demand, income and population growth explain many of the changes in during the past decade. Table 2.26 sets out key demand and supply factors by region to help evaluate the changes which have been taking place. The first five columns are demand-related and show sharp differences between the LDCs and OECD countries. The population growth figure for

Table 2.26

SELECTED FACTORS AFFECTING NET REGIONAL FOOD DEMAND

	Annual Average Growth 1970-1980 (per cent)			Income elasticities		Average Annual Growth of Agricultural GDP 1970-1980 (per cent)	Index of Food Production Per Capita in 1978-80 (1969-71 = 100)
	Population	Urban Population	GDP	Total Calories	Animal Calories		
OECD	.9	1.6	3.3	.07	.21	1.5	111
EEC-9	.4	.8	2.8	.08(1)	.28(1)	1.6	114
EFTA	.5	1.7	2.5			.6	104
Other Western Europe	1.5	3.3	4.7	.09(2)	.50(2)	2.7	118
United States	1.0	1.5	3.0	-.01	.02	1.2	115
Canada	1.1	1.7	2.9	.00	.15	2.8	109
Japan	1.1	2.1	5.0	.13	.46	1.1	93
Australia/New Zealand	1.4	1.9	2.9	.02	.05	1.7	120
LDCs	2.4	4.2	6.1	.35(5)	.70(5)	2.7	102
Geographic Groupings							
Africa	2.7	5.6	4.8	.40(4)	.81(4)	1.3	90
North	2.7	4.9	5.5	.40(2)	.73(2)	2.6	93
Southern	2.7	5.8	4.3	.39(3)	.94(3)	.9	89
Latin America	2.5	3.9	5.6	.19(2)	.40(2)	3.5	109
Western Asia	3.6	6.4	10.9	.42(2)	.85(2)	3.7	102
Eastern Asia	2.3	3.8	6.2	.32(3)	1.03(3)	2.9	104
Economic Groupings							
OPEC	2.6	4.5	7.7	.48(3)	.85(3)	2.4	99
NICs	2.3	4.0	6.4	.19(3)	.63(3)	3.4	115
Poorest LDCs	2.3	4.2	4.0	.38(4)	.93(4)	1.7	99

1. EEC-6.
2. Median value.
3. Median value based on random sample.
4. Per capita GDP used to obtain a weighted average.

Source: World Bank Development Report and FAO Agricultural Commodity projections, 1970-80, Vol. II, Rome 1971. Figures for regional groupings are weighted averages except where specified otherwise. Population is used to weight columns 1, 2 and 7 and GDP is used to weight columns 3 and 6.

- 53 -

all LDCs is more than two and a half times that of OECD countries which indicates that merely the maintenance of per capita food consumption levels will require a much faster increase in food supplies than in OECD countries. Perhaps more significant to OECD food exporters is the change in consumer food consumption patterns resulting from the rapid rate of urban population growth which is also taking place in LDCs. Urban consumers tend to purchase a higher proportion of products made from imported cereals than people in the more self-sufficient rural areas.

2.64. Income growth statistics in column 3 also reveal a much more rapid rate of growth in developing countries than in OECD countries. Western Asia, in particular, has witnessed very rapid growth in income in the past decade as a result of petroleum price increases.

2.65. Yet income growth provides only half of the demand picture. The increase in consumer food purchases resulting from a given increase in income depends on the initial level of consumers' incomes. The income elasticities for total calorie and animal calorie demand show that, in OECD countries where per capita incomes are high, consumers have a very small response to increases in income[28]. LDC consumers, on the other hand, increase consumption of calories by 24 per cent and of animal calories by 67 per cent for every 100 per cent increase in income. Hence a much larger proportion of income increases is spent on food in LDCs than in OECD countries. The high LDC demand elasticity for animal calories explains much of the growth of OECD exports of feedgrains, oilseeds, meat and dairy products to those countries in the past decade.

2.66. On the supply side, the growth of agricultural GDP in LDCs as a group has outperformed the OECD countries agricultural growth. Yet the slow growth of population as well as the low income elasticities of demand in OECD countries have allowed food production per capita (column 7) to increase in OECD countries. In the LDCs, the relatively high rate of increase in income has resulted in food demand growth in excess of the capability of LDC agricultural sectors to produce. The index of food production per capita has either remained the same or decreased in all LDC regions except for Latin America and East Asia where it increased by only 9 and 4 per cent over a ten-year period.

2.67. Data in Table 2.26 summarise the major changes which have taken place in the underlying structural determinants of agricultural trade which have been identified in Chapters I and II. They show why, for example, West Asia has become an important new market for Australian meat exports and why the poorest LDCs, with their slow income growth, have not been a very important force on world agricultural markets. Yet the effect of these structural determinants is influenced by policies. Policies reinforce or reduce the effect of the structural determinants; policies also redirect trade flows by making trade between particular trading countries more favourable than in the absence of such policy measures.

2.68. In addition to considering supply and demand factors by region as was presented in Table 2.26 and the related paragraphs, it is also interesting to consider OECD/LDC agricultural trade on a per capita basis. Table 2.27 based on data which has been adjusted for changes in unit values, provides additional information on a per capita basis concerning total trade and agricultural trade between OECD countries and (a) the rest of the world and (b) the developing countries as a group. As the table shows, the per capita trade data for the EFTA, the EEC and Canada are substantially above the per capita data for other selected countries and for the OECD as a whole. Total exports to the developing countries are greatest for the EEC, the U.S. and Japan; while Japan, the EEC and Australia/New Zealand, respectively, lead in exports per capita. The EEC, the U.S. and Japan are substantial importers, and imports per capita are greatest for Japan. Concerning agricultural trade with developing countries, the U.S. and the EEC are leaders in total trade ($4.9 billion and $4.4 billion respectively), while per capita agricultural exports are dominated by Australia/New Zealand

Table 2.27

SELECTED INDICATORS OF AGRICULTURAL TRADE PER CAPITA WITH DEVELOPING COUNTRIES

	OECD* 1972	OECD* 1980	EEC-9 1972	EEC-9 1980	EFTA 1972	EFTA 1980	United States 1972	United States 1980	Canada 1972	Canada 1980	Australia/New Zealand 1972	Australia/New Zealand 1980	Japan 1972	Japan 1980
Total trade with rest of the world														
Exports (US$ per capita)	387.3	1 521.4	283.0	1 150.0	680.0	2 749.4	227.6	915.9	924.1	2 610.5	465.4	1 335.0	266.7	1 109.3
Imports (US$ per capita)	400.0	1 716.4	280.9	1 375.3	795.3	3 319.8	264.5	1 099.4	864.9	2 406.7	371.1	1 411.5	219.0	1 197.8
Total agricultural trade														
Exports (US$ per capita)	49.2	174.8	21.8	95.8	46.0	129.3	41.6	165.7	119.1	324.4	201.9	551.4	6.5	14.6
Imports (US$ per capita)	61.6	184.8	59.7	165.0	86.2	257.5	36.2	90.4	68.0	179.5	23.9	76.4	40.6	144.3
Total trade with developing countries														
Exports (US$ billion)	50.3	284.3	19.8	111.1	2.8	14.9	13.0	75.8	1.3	6.7	1.5	7.0	10.8	58.7
(US$ per capita)	66.9	353.9	77.6	425.2	70.0	360.9	61.9	333.1	58.5	281.3	90.9	391.4	101.0	502.3
Imports (US$ billion)	57.7	412.3	26.4	154.2	2.7	17.6	14.1	117.8	1.6	7.7	0.8	6.4	9.7	84.4
(US$ per capita)	76.8	513.6	103.5	590.3	67.4	426.6	67.1	517.4	72.5	322.8	48.5	361.8	90.9	722.7
Agricultural trade with developing countries														
Exports (US$ billion)	6.0	34.7	1.9	12.4	0.2	0.8	2.4	13.7	0.3	1.7	0.8	3.5	0.2	1.1
(US$ per capita)	8.0	43.2	7.5	47.3	4.0	18.8	11.6	60.1	14.9	71.9	47.1	197.9	2.1	9.4
of which:														
Food grains & products														
(US$ billion)	2.1	9.9	0.3	2.4	0.0	0.0	1.2	4.6	0.2	1.1	0.3	1.2	0.0	0.3
(US$ per capita)	2.7	12.3	1.3	9.0	0.1	0.7	5.6	20.3	9.5	47.8	17.9	70.1	0.3	2.3
Feed grains & products														
(US$ billion)	0.3	4.1	0.1	0.6	0.0	0.0	0.2	3.0	0.0	0.1	0.0	0.2	0.0	0.0
(US$ per capita)	0.5	5.1	0.2	2.2	0.0	0.6	1.1	13.3	0.6	4.1	2.5	12.4	0.1	0.3
Imports (US$ billion)	13.7	43.5	6.3	20.3	0.9	2.7	4.1	12.0	0.3	0.9	0.1	0.5	1.4	4.9
(US$ per capita)	18.2	54.2	24.6	77.7	22.7	65.0	19.5	52.9	13.7	35.7	8.4	29.6	13.0	41.6
of which:														
Tropical beverages														
(US$ billion)	4.3	17.0	1.8	7.7	0.4	1.5	1.5	5.3	0.1	0.3	0.1	0.2	0.1	0.9
(US$ per capita)	5.7	21.1	7.2	29.5	9.8	36.3	7.2	23.2	5.2	12.6	4.5	14.1	1.2	7.6
Percentage share of agricultural trade with developing countries														
Exports	11.9	12.2	9.7	11.1	5.6	5.2	18.7	18.0	25.5	25.5	51.8	50.6	2.0	1.9
Imports	23.7	10.5	23.8	13.2	33.6	15.2	29.0	10.2	18.9	11.0	17.2	8.2	14.3	5.8

* Including Yugoslavia.

Note: Total trade = SITC 0-9.
Consult Table A3 in the Appendix for the SITC definition of agricultural trade and commodity groupings. Population data are as follows for each region or country, 1972 data, followed by 1980 data (in millions); OECD -- 752 and 803; EEC-9 -- 255 and 261; EFTA -- 40 and 41; USA -- 210 and 228; Canada -- 22 and 24; Australia/New Zealand -- 16 and 18; Japan -- 107 and 117.

Source: OECD Statistics of Foreign Trade, Series C.

at $71.2 per capita compared with $21.6 for the U.S. and $17.0 for the EEC. The U.S. and the EEC are leaders in the total value of exports of food grains and products; however Australia/New Zealand and Canada are predominant exporters in per capita terms. Per capita exports of feed grains are highest for Australia/New Zealand and the U.S. Total imports of food products are greatest for the EEC, the U.S. and Japan, although the EEC leads in per capita imports of food ($26.2) followed by the EFTA ($21.9) and the U.S. ($17.8). Agricultural exports as a percentage of total exports to developing countries in 1980 were as follows: Australia/New Zealand, 48.6 per cent; Canada, 24.5 per cent; U.S. 17.3 per cent; EEC, 10.7 per cent; OECD average 12.2 per cent, etc. These percentages were greater in 1980 than in 1972. Agricultural imports as a percentage of total imports in 1980 were greatest for the EFTA (17.3 per cent); the EEC (14.9 per cent); and the U.S. (11.6 per cent); OECD average, 11.9 per cent; these percentages were substantially below the 1972 levels.

Chapter III

THE EFFECT OF DOMESTIC AND TRADE POLICIES ON OECD-LDC AGRICULTURAL TRADE

I. PERSPECTIVES ON THE ROLE OF AGRICULTURAL TRADE BETWEEN OECD AND DEVELOPING COUNTRIES

3.1. The underlying structural determinants of agricultural trade, identified in the preceeding two chapters, are greatly influenced by the policies of trading nations. In order to understand how these policies have evolved and how they affect OECD-LDC agricultural trade, the context within which these policies have emerged must first be examined. It is especially important to distinguish between the role of food and agriculture in OECD countries and its role in LDCs. This distinction is responsible for differing policy objectives in OECD countries vis-à-vis the LDCs. This brief section attempts to highlight certain structural and economic factors and their interlinkages with policy initiatives in both the developed and developing countries.

3.2. Food and agriculture play a relatively much greater role in LDC economies than in OECD countries (Table 3.1). The first two rows of the table compare agriculture as a source of income in OECD countries with "low income" and "middle income" LDCs. In terms of both its share of GDP and as a source of employment, agriculture is far more important in LDCs than in OECD countries. The role of agriculture in the middle income group, however, is much smaller than for the low income group. The share of GDP in middle income LDCs is 15 per cent compared with 36 per cent in the low income countries and the proportion of the labour force in agriculture is only 44 per cent in the former compared with 71 per cent in the latter. Agriculture as a source of income declines as the development process proceeds.

3.3. Similar differences among the three groups of countries emerge when food consumption expenditures are compared (row 3). Consumer expenditures on food are nearly two thirds of consumer budgets in the low income countries and comprise almost half of consumer budgets in the middle income group while OECD consumers spend an average of only 28 per cent of their incomes on food. Food, and the price consumers have to pay for it, is vitally important to LDCs and has become the focus of the LDC approach to food and agriculture in the majority of countries.

3.4. The distinction between OECD countries and LDCs in agricultural trade is not as sharp as the differences in the structure of their food and agricultural sectors. The low income LDCs show a much greater dependence on imports and exports of food and agricultural products than the OECD countries. Yet the export and import shares of food and agricultural products for the middle income LDCs are almost identical to the shares for OECD. This is an indication

Table 3.1

COMPARATIVE INDICATORS FOR FOOD AND AGRICULTURE IN
THE OECD AND DEVELOPING COUNTRIES.

		OECD	LDCs "Low" income	LDCs "Middle" income
1.	Proportion of GDP from agriculture, 1980	4	36	15
2.	Percentage of labour force in agriculture, 1980	6	71	44
3.	Proportion of consumers' expenditure on food, beverages and tobacco, 1977	28	62	47
4.	Food and agricultural raw materials as a percentage of total exports, 1979	15	42	15
5.	Food as a percentage of total imports, 1979	12	17	11

Note: For items 1,2,4 and 5 see general note to Table 1.7. For item 3 the proportion given is the median value for a representative sample of countries in each group. See technical appendix for the criterion used to separate low and middle income LDCs.

Sources: The World Bank, World Development Report, 1982, Washington, D.C. [items 1,2,4 and 5]. U.N. Yearbook of National Accounts Statistics, 1979, Vols. I and II, New York [item 3]

of the importance of manufacturing exports for some countries and, oil exports for others in the middle income group.

3.5. The aggregated groupings in Table 3.1, however, tend to mask the importance of agricultural trade for particular countries. Table 3.2 shows both the relative importance of certain LDCs in relation to selected world commodity markets as well as the significance of those markets for their export earnings. The countries which are highly dependent on the exports of a particular commodity for their foreign exchange earnings are mostly in the lower income group and they usually do not have a significant share of the world market. (The exceptions are Colombia for coffee, Ghana for cocoa and Sri Lanka for tea.) The single commodity dependence of these countries makes their national incomes far more susceptible to price fluctuations in that commodity than are incomes of more developed countries with diversified economies.

3.6. Development is associated with an increased dispersion of economic activity and the diversification of exports. Countries such as Brazil (coffee and cocoa) and Thailand (rice) have large shares of major world commodity markets – a market pre-eminence which they

Table 3.2

THE IMPORTANCE OF SELECTED AGRICULTURAL COMMODITY EXPORTS
FOR DEVELOPING COUNTRIES

	Per cent of world market (1)	Per cent of total country exports (2)
Coffee		
LDC total	92	3.0
Brazil	17	
Colombia	15	63
El Salvador		63
Guatemala		43
Burundi		89
Eq. Guinea		45
Ethiopia		72
Madagascar		42
Rwanda		78
Uganda		93
Cocoa		
LDC total	95	1.0
Brazil	15	
Ghana	23	69
Ivory Coast	18	
Nigeria	16	
Tea		
LDC total	79	0.4
India	27	
Sri Lanka	22	46
Rice		
LDC total	45	0.5
Thailand	18	
Nepal		44
Sugar		
LDC total	38	0.8
Belize		48
Mauritius		66
Reunion		83
Swaziland		46
Fiji		55
Bananas		
LDC total	93	0.3
Costa Rica	13	
Ecuador	17	
Honduras	14	
Martinique		52
Cotton		
LDC total	48	0.9
Chad		78
Mali		44
Sudan		57
Yemen A.R.		41

1. Only shares greater than 10 per cent of the world market are shown.

2. Only shares greater than 40 per cent of total country exports are shown.

Source: World Bank Commodity Trade and Price Trends, August 1981, Tables 10 and 11.

Table 3.3

SIGNIFICANCE OF MANUFACTURED EXPORTS
FOR DEVELOPING COUNTRIES

	Average annual growth rate		Manufactured exports as a proportion of total exports (1979)	Destination of manufactured exports as % total (1979)	
	Agriculture	Manufacturing		OECD	LDCs
OECD	1.4	3.2	75	67	25
Low Income LDCs	2.2	3.7	42	43	47
Middle income LDCs	2.9	6.4	74	63	29

Note: See general note to Table 1.7.

Source: The World Bank, World Development Report 1982, Washington D.C.

have held for many years – but, as they have developed their industrial bases, the relative importance of these traditional commodity exports has declined.

3.7. Table 3.3 compares the role of manufactured exports with agricultural exports for low income and middle income LDCs. The growth rates for both the agricultural and the manufacturing sectors in the low income countries are below those for the middle income group. The 6.4 per cent growth rate for the manufacturing sector of the middle income LDCs is linked closely to the growing role of manufactured exports which accounted for 74 per cent of all middle income LDC exports compared to only a 42 per cent share of exports for the low income LDCs. The last two columns in the table show that OECD countries are proportionately much more important as destinations for middle income LDC manufactured exports than they are as destinations for low income LDCs. Only 43 per cent of low income LDC manufactured goods exports go to OECD countries compared with 63 per cent for the middle income LDCs. This reflects the growing importance to developing countries of access to OECD markets for manufactured products as they reach higher levels of development.

3.8. The data presented show that developing countries, in general, have a much greater degree of dependence on agriculture than OECD countries. However, there are wide differences among LDCs. Table 3.4 shows the widely differing agricultural import and export structures of four selected countries. A comparison of the mix of agricultural imports of Egypt and South Korea reflect sharp differences in their income levels and economic structures. Foodgrains account for a large proportion of both countries' imports from the OECD but feedgrains and oilseeds together make up 31.6 per cent of South Korean agricultural imports compared to only 7.0 per cent for Egypt. Also significant is the value of the agriculural raw materials imported from the OECD by the two countries ($288 million for Egypt compared to $1 217 million for South Korea). The higher figure for South Korea reflects the demands of the manufacturing sector for cotton, hides, skins and other products for processing and re-export.

Table 3.4

COMPARISON OF THE IMPORTS AND EXPORTS STRUCTURES OF AGRICULTURAL PRODUCTS FOR SELECTED LDCs IN 1980

	Imports from OECD					Exports to OECD			
	Egypt		South Korea		Ghana		Argentina	
Product groups	Value Mill.$	Percentage	Value Mill.$	Percentage	Value Mill.$	Percentage	Value Mill.$	Percentage
Foodgrains and Preparations	1 033.6	50.1	696.2	45.8	0.2	0.0	32.5	1.2
Feedgrains and other feeds (except oilmeals)	144.7	7.0	318.6	21.0	2.1	0.4	269.9	10.3
Oilseeds and meals	0.2	0.0	160.4	10.6	0.4	0.0	846.4	32.4
Dairy products and eggs	148.2	7.2	6.0	0.4	0.0	0.0	6.6	0.3
Live animals and meat	208.8	10.1	19.5	1.3	0.0	0.0	746.9	28.6
Fruit and vegetables	42.0	2.0	17.6	1.2	2.0	0.3	233.1	8.9
Sugar, preparations and honey	96.1	4.6	96.6	6.4	0.0	0.0	127.8	4.9
Coffee, tea, cocoa, juices and preparations	6.9	0.3	3.5	0.2	576.3	96.9	22.4	0.9
All food items	2 064.8	100.0	1 519.5	100.0	594.5	100.0	2 615.3	100.0
Raw materials of agricultural origin	288.2		1 217.0		60.6		344.2	
All products	8 226.3		12 232.8		1 033.0		4 128.2	

NOTE: OECD includes Yugoslavia and Intra-EEC trade.

Source: OECD Statistics of Foreign Trade, Series C; See Appendix Table A.3 for SITC product definitions.

3.9. The export structures of the two exporting LDCs show the difference between a small tropical product exporter (Ghana) and a large diversified exporter (Argentina) whose products compete with those of OECD countries. Ghana's exports of tropical beverages accounted for almost all of its agricultural exports and $594 million of its total $1 033 million in foreign exchange earnings in 1980. Argentine agricultual exports to the OECD on the other hand, comprise a similar proportion of the country's total exports but include a greater variety of products including feedgrains, oilseeds, meat, fruits and vegetables and sugar.

3.10. The evidence presented suggests that it is better to view LDCs *not* as a single group of countries with relatively homogeneous needs but as an economically diverse group at different stages of the development process. This diversity, and the differing needs and objectives of a wide range of developing countries, should be recognised by policy-makers.

3.11. A second factor which emerges is the increase in the importance of the manufacturing sector – and, hence, of manufactured exports – to LDCs as they move along the path of development. Access to OECD markets for manufactured goods is critical to the development of the LDCs since the size of their markets for these goods is not sufficient to sustain large sophisticated internationally competitive industries. As these industries grow within LDCs, they generate income and, as a consequence, growing markets for OECD exports. A recent GATT publication shows that, after excluding trade within Western Europe and between the United States and Canada, 48 per cent of industrial country exports went to developing countries – 31 per cent to the non-oil exporting LDCs and 17 per cent to the oil exporters[29].

3.12. Finally, in spite of the diversity among LDCs and the growing importance of the manufacturing sector associated with higher levels of development, the underlying structure of LDC economies is sufficiently different from that of OECD countries to produce an approach to agricultural policy which is distinct, in very general terms, from the approach of most OECD members. The following section examines the major thrusts of OECD and LDC agricultural policies and how they affect OECD-LDC agricultural trade. It is these underlying forces and structures which tend to reinforce, weaken or in some way fashion policy initiatives in OECD countries and also in the developing countries. The following section also examines the relationships behind the economic interdependence of the OECD countries and the developing countries.

II. THE POLICY APPROACH TO AGRICULTURE AND TRADE

3.13. The recent study on *Problems of Agricultural Trade* concluded that:
- Interdependence between the agricultural sector and the whole economy must be recognised if an open trading system on a global basis is to be maintained and developed;
- Recognition must be given to the strong relationships which exist between national policies and international agricultural trade.

Any consideration of trading relationships must therefore begin with an understanding of the underlying domestic policy framework and how it has been designed to meet the diverse, sometimes conflicting, objectives associated with the food and agricultural sector.

3.14. A broad analytical framework is constructed in this section drawing upon many common objectives and policy elements which characterise each of the two groups of countries under consideration. The general agricultural policy approach of the OECD vis-à-vis the LDCs provides the background for specific policy analysis which follows.

A. The OECD Approach to Agriculture and Trade

3.15. The policy objectives of OECD countries discussed in previous OECD studies[30] include priorities such as greater productivity and efficiency in the farm sector; promotion of greater food security; the stabilization of supplies, and environmental and regional concerns.

3.16. A number of measures are employed by Member countries to promote these objectives. A recent OECD study on trade indicated that while it may not always be possible to accurately quantify their effects on trade it should be possible to qualitatively identify the links with trade and trade performance and to make the interaction more transparent. Policy objectives and the measures through which they are carried out can have direct or indirect effects on trade. Direct effects are easily recognisable; indirect effects on trade can often not be singled out[31]. With this in mind it is apparent that the ultimate effect of the various measures used by Member countries is to improve sector welfare through direct and indirect transfers of resources from other sectors of the economy. Some of these transfers result from public sector investments in research and infra-structure which improve efficiency and allow countries to exploit their natural supply potential. In general, these measures improve market transparency, and enhance the functioning of the market. Other measures result in large transfers of income to the rural sector which, even though they are done with specific social objectives in mind, may cause price distortions which inhibit the functioning of the market.

3.17. In most OECD countries, price and other support programmes for agriculture have the effect of increasing agricultural output. For exporters, this results in higher export availability. For importers, it results in reduced demand for imports. Both effects contribute to lowering prices on world markets for the products affected and for their substitutes.

3.18. There are, however, other sets of policies which work in the opposite direction. Some exporting countries, rather than allowing exports to increase automatically when domestic output rises, purchase and store the additional production in the short to medium-term and use incentive payments to control production in order to limit the build-up of stocks. In other cases, production and hence export availability is reduced through the reduction of producer prices to reflect the reductions in export prices. These policies reduce the dampening effect of domestic support programmes upon world market prices. Other things being equal, they contribute to reduced export availability and ultimately higher export prices.

3.19. The accumulation of stocks has the effect of contributing to market stability by creating a buffer against world production shortfalls due to weather conditions. Government purchases of these products are often used in concessional sales, food aid programmes, or for disaster relief. These programmes contribute to stability and world food security objectives. On the other hand, "to varying degrees all (OECD) governments apply policies based on support and protection, mainly to compensate for low farm incomes and the effects of unstable international commodity markets"[32]. For certain commodities these policies are often in the form of border measures which often have the ultimate effect of providing a marked degree of market insulation vis-à-vis the international market for these commodities. "While the autonomous imposition of border measures may be effective in providing means for modifying the effects of world market fluctuations so that interior adjustment is kept within desirable limits, the international repercussions of such actions generally provoke world market adjustment[33]. What is relevant for instability in the international market is the extent to which domestic events transfer instability to the international market and thence to other market participants"[34], whether they are OECD countries or developing countries. (See also paragraphs 3.55 and 3.57).

3.20. In the final analysis, OECD agricultural and trade policies tend to reinforce the underlying trends identified at the end of the last chapter. Policies have increased the quantities of temperate agricultural products available to world markets, resulting in a redirection of some trade flows and a reduction in the general level of world prices.

B. The LDC Approach to Agriculture and Trade

3.21. The developing countries, as a group, have taken a rather different approach (compared to OECD countries) to food and agricultural policies. The reasons for this approach are much the same as the reasons underlying the growth in LDC agricultural imports identified in Chapter II. It stems from a more agriculture-oriented economic base, lower consumer purchasing power relative to the OECD, and large rural populations which, in many cases, are migrating rapidly to urban areas. It also reflects differing (often undeveloped and sometimes unstable) political institutions. The policy emphasis is often on transforming society from rural agrarian to one which is urban and industrial.

3.22. The large, diverse rural populations and the proportionately small but politically vocal groups of urban consumers make it politically and economically impractical for most LDCs to provide the support to the agricultural sector which exists in most OECD countries. Instead, the flow of resources is usually from the agricultural sector to the urban industrial sector. In effect, agricultural production is often taxed in order to favour the urban consumer.

3.23. Foodgrains, including maize, millet and sorghum, are traditionally the focus of LDC food and agricultural policies but major export commodities often also come under strict regulation. One of the most common approaches used by developing countries is some form of retail price control or subsidies for the consumption of basic food staples. A recent study on Sub-Saharan Africa showed, for example, that 31 of the 40 developing countries included in the study had some form of retail price control on at least one domestic food crop[35]. Other major LDCs which have, or until recently have had, retail price controls include Egypt (bread), India (wheat), Pakistan (wheat), Thailand (rice) and Indonesia (rice). Governments may also provide an indirect subsidy to consumers by controlling imports or restricting exports so that domestic prices are reduced below those prevailing on the world market.

3.24. In spite of the predominant emphasis on providing "cheap" food to urban consumers, many LDCs have made great strides in their agricultural development and productivity. Investment in irrigation and the introduction of hybrid seeds have helped India to become self-sufficient in wheat after being one of the world's largest importers in the 1960s. Cameroon's commitment to peasant agriculture has allowed the country's agricultural production to grow at an average annual rate of 4 per cent from 1960 to 1980 – in sharp contrast to trends in the rest of the continent[36].

3.25. The group of newly industrialized countries are another exception to the tendency of LDCs to support consumers at the expense of agriculture. Government revenues generated in the industrial sector allow these countries to shift some support to the agricultural sector. In some cases this means government support for agriculture through producer prices which are above world levels, and for urban consumers via lowered retail prices; in other cases the support for consumers has been abandoned in favour of support for the agricultural sector.

3.26. Whether a Government exercises direct control of the market through the buying and selling of foodgrains or whether its control is predominantly indirect through the use of taxes and trade restrictions, the ultimate effect is to lower producer prices and hence, cost-effectiveness of investment and income from agricultural employment relative to other opportunities. These policies, therefore, provide an additional stimulus to rural-urban migration. In the rural sector, investment in agriculture is decreased. Producers may shift from food crop to cash crop production or they may remain entirely outside the national marketing system producing only enough to meet their own basic needs.

C. Overall Effect of OECD and LDC Agricultural Policy Approaches

3.27. An increased reliance by developing countries on imports for supplies of agricultural products may have tended to occur naturally, due to the relatively rapid increase in their food demand resulting from income and population growth. The underlying policy approaches currently being pursued in both groups of countries, however, tend to reinforce the trend towards increasing LDC dependence on imports, particularly from OECD countries.

3.28. This is brought out in Table 3.5 which indicates some aspects of the degree of protection in selected countries for wheat, maize and rice, calculated by the OECD Secretariat based on average prices received by producers in 1978. The data illustrate the difference between world market prices and domestic producer and consumer prices caused by trade restrictions and other measures which separate domestic from international prices. This allows for a measurement of the impact of agricultural and trade policies on the prices paid and received by consumers and producers respectively. A comparison of the consumer figure with the producer figure also indicates the extent to which one group is being required to support the other. For example, if the ad valorem tariff equivalent is positive and the same for both consumers and producers, the cost of producer price support is being fully borne by consumers. Where the figures for consumers and producers differ, the government – i.e. taxpayers – account for the balance.

3.29. All the importing OECD countries given in the table have positive tariff equivalents for both consumers and producers for all three grains. In some cases (e.g. Japan and Greece for wheat and Spain for maize), the rates for consumers are below those for producers indicating that consumers do not have to bear all of the producer price support.

3.30. Importing LDCs have a mixture of policies which result in effects ranging from support for producers to support for consumers and even support for both. The lower income LDCs – Egypt, India, Pakistan and Indonesia – have negative tariff equivalents which mean that consumers can purchase the relevant grain at subsidised prices and producers receive prices which are below world levels.

3.31. The newly industrialised countries represent countries in transition in terms of their agricultural policy approach. South Korea shows a strong positive level of support for producers in all three grains with at least some of this being borne by consumers. Brazil and Taiwan for wheat and Mexico for maize provide higher than world market prices for producers and lower than world market prices for consumers thereby subsidising both groups. Mexican wheat policies favour consumers as is reflected in the negative figures for both producers and consumers.

3.32. These figures, on balance, support the contention that trade policies in OECD countries tend to provide positive incentives to produce and export agricultural commodities while LDC policies tend to work in the opposite direction to reduce production incentives and increase the propensity to import. These policy effects, when combined with economic and structural forces pushing in the same direction, add further weight to the trend of growing LDC imports of OECD agricultural products.

Table 3.5

AD VALOREM TARIFF EQUIVALENT OF DIFFERENCES BETWEEN DOMESTIC AND
INTERNATIONAL PRICES FOR MAJOR GRAINS AT PRODUCER AND CONSUMER LEVELS, 1978

	Percentage by which domestic price is higher or lower (-) than world price for	
Commodity and Country	Producers	Consumers
Soft Wheat		
Importing OECD		
EEC	97.3	97.3
Greece	54.9	30.9
Japan	442.8	59.5
Spain	34.2	34.2
Importing LDCs		
Brazil	53.0	-42.0
Egypt	-39.0	-71.1
India	-7.0	-19.5
S. Korea	167.3	4.8
Mexico	-8.6	-21.1
Pakistan	-33.8	-42.5
Taiwan	81.5	-17.5
Exporting OECD		
Australia	-5.5	-6.0
United States (1)	-14.4	-14.4
Exporting LDC		
Argentina	-5.5	-5.5
Corn		
Importing OECD		
EEC	114.9	114.9
Greece	55.8	-
Spain	80.5	67.4
Importing LDCs		
S. Korea	184.3	9.8
Mexico	5.8	-14.5
Taiwan	81.9	5.8
Exporting OECD		
United States (2)	-16.3	-16.3
Exporting LDC		
Argentina	-5.5	-5.5
Rice (3)		
Importing OECD		
EEC	85.9	85.9
Importing LDCs		
S.Korea	113.8	87.0
Indonesia	-16.6	-17.0
Exporting OECD		
Japan	339.5	270.5
United States	-38.7	-38.7
Exporting LDCs		
Pakistan	-59.7	-59.7
Thailand	-36.7	-36.7

1. OECD computation using the season average price of wheat received by producers and the unit value of U.S. exports.

2. OECD computations using 1978 U.S. season average corn price received by farmers and the Gulf price of No. 2 yellow corn.

3. Quality differences have a relatively greater influence on rice prices than prices for other grains. Hence a larger proportion of the difference between domestic and world prices may be attributed to quality differences than is the case for wheat or maize.

Source: Due to differences in price data available among countries, domestic prices used to calculate the differences may not be strictly comparable. Calculations were made by the Secretariat based on the method used in: C.L. Jabara, Trade Restrictions in International Grain and Oilseed Markets, "A Comparative Country Analysis"; USDA, FAER, Report, No. 162, January 1981.

III. AGRICULTURAL TRADE POLICIES

3.33. The discussion of the general thrust of OECD and LDC policies above, ignored many of the trade issues associated with particular countries or groups of countries and with particular commodities. This section examines OECD and LDC agricultural policies in more detail and identifies and analyses selected policies pursued by these countries. It is divided into two parts: a) national policies pursued unilaterally by sovereign governments (with the EEC considered as a national entity), and b) multilateral policies pursued jointly by a number of countries.

A. National Policies

3.34. Two possible effects can be associated with a trade policy measure. One is to affect aggregate world trade volume in aggregate, i.e. on the size of the world market. The second is an effect on the pattern of trade flows in the world market without affecting the total volume of trade. All policies tend to have both effects but some policies, such as tariffs, quotas and other measures which limit access by all countries to a given market, largely affect the total size of the international market rather than the trade among particular countries. Other policies such as embargoes, bilateral agreements, aids to facilitate exports, voluntary trade restrictions etc., also effect the total volume of trade but in addition they have a more direct impact on the pattern of trade flows. This is an important distinction. Changes in the total volume of trade will have an important effect on the level and stability of prices. Changes in the pattern of trade flows, however, may only affect the relationship between particular trading countries while having only negligible effects on other traders in the market.

3.35. This section focuses on measures affecting the size and stability of the market. Even though policies which are designed to affect trade flows are becoming increasingly important as a means of dealing with trade issues, the effects of these measures are unclear and difficult to measure. Data and documentation are difficult to obtain for all but the most prominent of these policies.

1. *Policies of OECD Countries and their Implications for the Developing Countries*

3.36. Many of the issues and problems which are contentious among OECD countries are also the focus of disputes in OECD-LDC agricultural trade. The OECD Study on *Problems of Agricultural Trade* examined these problems in detail and they need not be discussed again in this study. Instead the emphasis will be on those aspects which are unique to OECD-LDC agricultural trade.

a) *Effects on Developing Country Exporters*

3.37. OECD agricultural policies affect different LDCs in a variety of ways. Generalisations can easily obscure policy effects which may have dramatic effects in a small, single-export-commodity-based LDC while having virtually little or no effect on the world market or on the OECD country from which the policy change originates. Nevertheless, a broad overview is required to clarify the effects of the various types of policies. Major policy effects must be identified and their principal implications understood with the realisation that some countries may not fit in the general pattern.

3.38. OECD agricultural and trade policies affect LDC exporters primarily by restricting their market access. The restriction of market access by OECD countries – as with all countries – is primarily an extension of domestic agricultural policies. Hence the level of intended domestic support for agricultural products is roughly associated with the degree of domestic market insulation required to prevent competition from foreign sources. Table 3.5 has provided an indication of differing levels of domestic support (for consumers and producers) as measured by the differences in domestic and world price levels in 1978 for selected grains. These measurements are only an approximation of domestic support but they do indicate, at least, the general thrust of domestic policies and the degree of domestic market insulation which is likely to be required to maintain these price differences.

3.39. Separation in the domestic and world market is usually achieved through tariffs, levies and a wide variety of non-tariff barriers (NTBs). These measures are employed to varying degrees by many countries for certain categories of LDC exports – in particular, sugar, meats, fruits, vegetables, oils, and protein-rich supplements for feedstuffs. The most prevalent NTBs are export subsidies, countervailing duties, import licensing, state trading, seasonal import bans, voluntary export restrictions, explicit quotas, variable levies, sanitary regulations, and size and quality regulations. These measures, however, are not unique to OECD countries; they are applied widely among developing countries as well (see paragraphs 3.59 – 3.61).

3.40. Often high levels of producer prices (in cereals and other commodities) in OECD countries are coupled with high levels of protection which stimulate domestic production and hinder access to these markets by exporting countries. If production exceeds domestic utilisation and normal stocks, surpluses begin to accumulate. One of the most common outlets for these surpluses is the world market where subsidies or restitutions are required to make the commodity in domestic surplus competitive. The net effect of such export aids is to (*a*) lower world prices and (*b*) alter trade flows and export shares vis-à-vis exporting countries who do not promote their exports in a comparable way.

3.41. A recent study has estimated the benefits to developing countries of a reduction in OECD agricultural trade restrictions[37]. The study assumes a 50 per cent reduction in OECD agricultural trade barriers in 1977, which increases revenues to exporting countries from two sources: an increase in the volume exported as foreign suppliers displace marginal domestic OECD producers; and the increase in world prices which results from the lower level of subsidised OECD production. The study finds that world agricultural exports would increase by about $8.5 billion per year (in 1977 dollars), of which approximately 36 per cent would accrue to the 56 LDCs selected for the study, 20 per cent would go to OECD exporters and the remainder, 44 per cent, would accrue to a rest-of-the-world category which includes smaller LDCs and centrally planned countries. Among the LDCs, Latin America receives approximately 60 per cent of the total (LDC) benefits, Asia receives 23 per cent, and North Africa/Middle East and Sub-Saharan Africa receive approximately 9 per cent each.

3.42. The study shows that all agricultural exporting countries are likely to benefit from a substantial reduction in OECD agricultural protection, hence some of these benefits would accrue to OECD Members who are predominant exporters of certain commodities. Among the LDCs, most of the benefits accrue to the higher income LDCs in Latin America. The poorest LDCs in Sub-Saharan Africa benefit very little as a group.

3.43. Two additional observations can be made about the effect of a hypothetical reduction in OECD agricultural protection. The changes in LDC export and import revenues and products affected in Table 3.6 show that the benefits vary widely from country to country and that some countries (e.g. Bangladesh, Egypt, Venezuela) are actually net losers. The reason is that, these countries either export few agricultural products and/or export commodities (currently) facing low rates of protection (such as jute from Bangladesh) and at the same time import foods bearing high rates of protection in the OECD for which world market prices are estimated to increase when protection is reduced.

3.44. The second observation to emerge from the table is that most of the LDC gains can be attributed to a few product groups. In fact, four products (raw sugar, refined sugar, beef and veal and green coffee) out of the 99 included in the study account for 50 per cent of the increase in LDC export revenues.

3.45. The results of this study suggest that, in the final analysis and notwithstanding its other merits, a broad reduction in OECD agricultural trade restrictions may have little impact on the least developed countries. Trade liberalisation can be an important stimulus to development, but liberalisation by OECD countries only and for agricultural commodities only, is unlikely (by itself) to adequately address the production/marketing problems endemic to many developing countries. Such problems must be addressed by more specific policy measures undertaken by both OECD and LDC countries simultaneously.

3.46. Trade restrictions on agricultural trade per se cover a wide range of measures including tariff and non-tariff barriers. During the 1970s OECD countries have made significant progress in reducing (and in some cases eliminating) tariffs applied to imports of raw and semi-processed agricultural products from developing countries. These reductions have, however, been less for agricultural products than for industrial products. However it should be recognised that tariff reductions vary according to the stage of processing and that agricultural exports by LDCs often involve raw or semi-processed commodities. According to research conducted by the GATT[38], an overall tariff average for agricultural products is difficult to calculate since many commodities are also affected by non-tariff measures. The data presented below are tariff reduction averages calculated on items on which concessions were exchanged during the Tokyo Round. Tariff reductions on both a weighted and simple basis which were agreed upon in the Tokyo Round were as follows:

	Tariff Average %		Rate of reduction %
	Pre-MTN	Post-MTN	
ALL Industrial (weighted)	7.5	5.5	26
Products (simple)	10.3	6.5	37
Agricultural (weighted)	7.9	6.9	12
Products (simple)	11.7	11.0	7

However it is also recognised that OECD countries employ a variety of multilateral (and national) measures, schemes and incentives to promote the expansion of LDC exports to OECD Member countries (see paragraphs 3.78 – 3.120). As a further example the Generalised System of Preferences (GSP) is an important multilateral scheme whereby tariff preferences are given to beneficiary countries (see paragraphs 3.105 – 3.110). For example as Table 3.12 demonstrates, in 1980 agricultural imports accorded GSP as a percentage of dutiable imports (column 6) amounted to the following percentages according to the importing country: Austria, 18.6; Finland, 16.3; Japan, 19.5; Sweden, 49.1; and Switzerland, 13.2.

3.47. The escalation of tariffs on processed products is particularly significant for LDC exporters. The development process typically requires a gradual evolution of a country's economic structure from agriculture to light industry to heavy and technically sophisticated industry. The processing of agricultural products for export is a natural first step in the evolution of many developing country economies. Trade barriers to processed products can be a significant impediment to growth in these developing economies. OECD countries, as major markets for processed goods, have a significant impact in this area although, as will be shown later LDCs themselves also have tariffs that escalate sharply with the level of processing.

b) *Effects on Developing Country Importers*

3.48. The effects of OECD countries' agricultural policies on the food-importing developing countries are equally as varied and complex as their effects on LDC exporters, discussed in the previous section. One of the major concerns of the importing countries as a group is food security (see also paragraphs 3.73 – 3.77). In addition to increasing domestic output, the attainment of this goal often concerns the availability of sufficient world supplies at attractive prices and/or at a low level of price variability. This section discusses the effect of OECD countries' policies on the instability of supplies and prices.

3.49. It has already been stated that one outcome of agricultural policies in OECD countries has been an expansion of production and export availability of certain temperate agricultural products with a consequent depressing effect on world prices, particularly for grains. This has allowed LDC importers to purchase food on world markets at prices below those which would have prevailed in the absence of OECD support policies. The IFPRI study (para. 3.41) partially quantified the effects of these policies by estimating the amount by which LDC import expenditures for food would increase given a 50 per cent reduction in OECD agricultural trade barriers for the year 1977. Column 2 of Table 3.6 shows that the increase in food import costs could be substantial and, as mentioned earlier, some LDCs may suffer a net decline in their agricultural trade balances as a result of lower OECD support for agriculture.

3.50. OECD policies affect not only the level of world food prices but also relative food prices. Such policies have stimulated the production and export of several commodities (e.g. cereals, dairy products, sugar etc.). Often, these exports have reinforced changing tastes and preferences (based on income growth and urbanisation) and sometimes displaced traditional food staples in the diets of consumers in developing countries. To the extent that this has occurred, LDCs have become more dependent on foreign sources for their food supplies (e.g. wheat).

3.51. OECD policies, however, are not the only factor affecting the change in diets of developing country consumers. Wheat products have a technical advantage in some LDCs where traditional staples require long preparation times in the home are not a suitable diet for urban consumers. Also, policies in many LDCs subsidise the consumption of wheat products. OECD policies have had very little effect on the diet in countries such as Egypt, Pakistan and India where wheat and wheat product prices are kept low through price controls and government regulation of domestic grain markets.

3.52. The functioning of international commodity markets as mentioned earlier is a major concern of the developing countries and is relevant to the issue of food security in these countries. Market instability is very complex, results from many factors and highlights the interdependence between the OECD countries and the developing countries. Price fluctuations are inherent in agricultural markets and to the extent that they reflect underlying changes in supply and demand, they are the natural results of market adjustments. This topic was dealt with at length in a 1980 OECD document[39]. As this Study, and the Study on Problems of Agricultural Trade demonstrated, domestic and agricultural trade policies can distort prices and prevent them from conveying a consistent message to all market participants.

Table 3.6

ESTIMATES OF THE POTENTIAL TRADE EFFECTS ON DEVELOPING COUNTRIES
FROM REDUCING TRADE BARRIERS TO AGRICULTURAL IMPORTS BY THE OECD COUNTRIES

Country	Change in Export Revenues	Change in Agricultural Import Expenditures	Increase in Agricultural Export Revenues	Most Affected Export Commodity in Absolute Terms
	(U.S.$1 000)		Per cent	
Sub-Saharan Africa				
Angola	11 623	-2 452	3.9	Coffee
Cameroon	21 391	-552	4.8	Cocoa
Ghana	31 152	-1 945	4.4	Cocoa
Guinea	245	-102	2.7	Coffee
Ivory Coast	49 581	-2 101	4.2	Cocoa
Kenya	18 415	-5 884	5.9	Beef
Madagascar	16 925	-1 185	8.4	Sugar
Malawi	9 686	-220	6.3	Beverages/tobacco
Mali	2 955	142	10.0	Vegetable oils
Mozambique	12 251	-1 219	17.1	Sugar
Niger	1 045	311	7.7	Vegetable oils
Nigeria	19 840	829	3.9	Cocoa
Rwanda	1 597	59	2.9	Coffee
Senegal	20 500	649	7.1	Vegetable oils
Tanzania	11 653	-4 371	5.8	Beef
Uganda	13 369	-64	3.1	Coffee
Upper Volta	195	-387	2.1	Pulses
Zaire	9 879	-4 802	4.3	Coffee
Zambia	943	-449	8.2	Beverages/tobacco
Asia				
Bangladesh	2 017	-5 511	5.3	Beverages/tobacco
Burma	6 344	-466	3.0	Rice
Hong Kong	723	-16 168	16.2	Fats
India	254 872	-181 576	18.4	Sugar
Indonesia	42 461	-29 256	6.1	Vegetable oils
Malaysia	49 314	3 626	6.4	Vegetable oils
Nepal	1 034	-605	2.3	Rice
Pakistan	14 850	-52 631	4.5	Beverages/tobacco
Philippines	154 356	-12 480	10.7	Sugar
South Korea	34 986	1 739	22.9	Sugar
Sri Lanka	14 841	3 823	4.1	Beverages/tobacco
Thailand	105 518	-106	6.6	Sugar
North Africa/Middle East				
Afghanistan	14 084	-291	32.8	Temperate fruits
Algeria	78 899	-34 873	28.5	Beverages/tobacco
Egypt	17 392	-63 160	12.4	Temperate fruits
Iran	190	-107 955	...	Temperate fruits
Iraq	914	-11 828	9.7	Wheat
Morocco	28 681	-17 810	10.1	Vegetable oils
Saudi Arabia	...	5 425	...	...
Sudan	6 947	-1 767	3.0	Oilseeds
Syria	4 933	-11 515	17.6	Coarse grains
Tunisia	35 944	-9 059	22.2	Vegetables oils
Turkey	81 026	-10 117	23.1	Beverages/tobacco
Yemen, Arab Republic of	156	2 618	5.1	Coffee
Latin America				
Argentina	568 009	1 516	17.3	Beef
Bolivia	14 508	-1 427	22.6	Sugar
Brazil	773 788	-20 584	12.8	Sugar
Chile	39 731	-10 949	40.1	Temperate fruits
Colombia	99 702	-3 109	8.5	Sugar
Dominican Republic	79 384	-1 194	11.7	Sugar
Ecuador	28 930	-652	5.8	Sugar
El Salvador	25 228	-38	5.8	Coffee
Guatemala	39 608	-2 088	7.6	Sugar
Haiti	5 572	-87	8.4	Sugar
Mexico	87 379	-46 810	16.8	Coffee
Peru	38 419	-5 819	14.1	Sugar
Venezuela	3 898	-39 816	5.9	Coffee

Note: Calculations use the base period 1975-77 for the 99 selected agricultural commodities only.

Source: A. Valdes and Joachim Zietz, Agricultural Protection in OECD Countries: Its Cost to Less-Developed Countries, IFPRI, December 1980.

3.53. As past OECD research (cited previously) and paragraph 3.19 have demonstrated, if market participants (both developed and developing) utilise greater flexibility in adjusting their internal markets to world price fluctuations, it is likely that short-term world price variability (and the adjustment required for each respective participant) will be lessened compared to a situation where domestic markets are insulated from price developments in international markets[40]. In achieving such market insulation (regardless of the rationale of individual governments i.e. food security, national defense, income support, protection of domestic sub-sectors etc.) there is an element of a "trade-off" at the expense of short-term market (price) stability on the world market. (This applies to developing as well as developed countries and to industrial sectors as well as to the agricultural sector.)

3.54. The effect that OECD trade restrictions have on world market stability depends on the types of measures employed and the importance of the country employing a particular restriction in the world market. Large trading countries with restrictive policies can have a significant impact on world price stability[41].

3.55. It must be emphasised, however, that OECD countries are probably not the major sources of world agricultural price instability – although this is an empirical question which would have to be tested. The state trading regimes in centrally planned countries and in most developing countries prevent the transmission of price fluctuations and thereby transmit all their domestic instability onto world markets. These countries also tend to have greater annual variations in agricultural production than do the OECD countries where capital intensity, hybrid seeds and effective farm management minimise the effects of weather. Finally, as large stockholders of grain, some major OECD grain exporters are an extremely important stabilizing force on world grain markets. Most developing countries hold only minimal stocks of grain relying implicitly on stocks held in OECD countries.

2. The Impact of LDC Policies on OECD Member Countries

3.56. The effects of OECD agrilcultural policies on LDCs have been examined and discussed at length in numrous articles and documents – some of which have already been cited. The examination of LDC agricultural and trade policies and their effects on OECD countries, as well as on other LDCs, has by comparison received very little attention. This is a particularly significant omission given the growing importance of LDCs in world agricultural markets as described in the preceding chapters. This section cannot completely redress this omission since published data and information on a broad range of LDC agricultural policies is far more limited than the material on OECD policies. Yet, these issues must be raised and discussed with the limited evidence available in order to provides a more balanced picture of OECD-LDC agricultural trade relations and their prospects for the future.

a) The Impact on OECD Exporters

3.57. The growth rates of agricultural imports presented earlier suggest that access to LDC agricultural markets is likely to be a question of increasing importance over the next 10 to 20 years. Earlier sections observed the tendency of many LDCs to subsidise consumers by fixing low food prices. These measures have tended to increase the demand for grain imports in LDCs as domestic production is discouraged and as consumers demand larger quantities of the subsidised grain. The effect on world markets – in contrast to the general effect of OECD policies – is to strengthen prices.

3.58. The fixing of internal prices in many LDCs has given rise to state trading regimes which are, in many ways, the most effective means of ensuring that the events in foreign markets do not interfere with domestic policy objectives.

3.59. State trading agencies are extremely effective in regulating the flow of a commodity into or out of a country as well as controlling the source of purchases or the destination of exports. Examples of state trading agencies and their function in some of the more important LDCs are as follows:

- Brazilian wheat imports are controlled by the Wheat Marketing Office of the Bank of Brazil (CTRIN) which has the sole authority for purchase and resale of all domestic and imported wheat. Imports are controlled through strict import licensing.
- Egyptian wheat imports are in the hands of the Ministry of Supply which has a monopoly on wheat and flour imports.
- The Food Corporation of India (FCI), a government agency, is the sole importer of wheat into India.
- The Korean Flour Industry Association (KOFMIA), a government sanctioned trade group, is the sole importer of wheat into Korea.
- Mexico's National Public Supply Company (CONSUPO) had a monopoly on coarse grains imports until 1979 when the private sector was allowed to play a more important role in grain imports. Mixed committees consisting of representatives from CONSUPO, the Ministry of Commerce and the appropriate private trade organisation now handle the purchase and import of all grains. These mixed committees still function in much the same way as a state trading agency.
- Indonesian rice imports are all channelled through BULOG, an independent government agency with the sole authority for import and domestic procurement of rice.

3.60. Information on many of the state trading agencies in the poorer, smaller trading LDCs is difficult to obtain. A recent study of the problems of Sub-Saharan Africa, however, found that 33 of the 38 countries in the study had some form of government or quasi-government marketing institution for one or more agricultural products[42]. Hence, state control of agricultural marketing and imports in LDCs is widespread.

3.61. State trading, per se, does not necessarily restrict trade. This will depend on how and to what degree prices are controlled and how the sources of supply are influenced by non-competitive factors. The primary effect of state trading – from the view-point of an OECD exporter – is that it controls access to a particular country's market and, as a result, the means by which access to the market is obtained is often unclear and subject to discretionary changes in government policy. For example, a World Bank study identified nine major changes in Nigerian rice trade policy (affecting tariff rates, import regulations, licensing and quantitative import restrictions) in a seven-year period from 1974 to 1980. The conclusion reached was that, "Erratic trade policy not only has a dramatic effect on price levels,... but also has increased the risk to traders..."[43].

3.62. In addition to less clearly defined restrictions on market access which result from the use of state trading regimes, LDCs make extensive use of tariffs, duties and other border measures. Table 3.7 compares the average ad valorem tariff rates of agricultural, industrial and total product categories for selected LDCs. Because these rates are arithmetic averages rather than weighted averages, and because they do not include all trade restrictions – such as non-tariff barriers – they must be viewed as an approximation to the degree of protection. Yet it is apparent that the rates of protection are very high for some countries. Most of the countries with rates of agricultural protection over 30 per cent – Tanzania, Uganda, Bangladesh, India, Pakistan, Sri Lanka, Egypt, Ghana, Morocco, Nigeria, South Korea, Philippines, Ecquador, Mexico and Venezuela – are extremely important in world agricultural markets.

Table 3.7

AVERAGE DUTY RATES IN SELECTED DEVELOPING COUNTRIES

Per Cent Ad Valorem Tariffs

Countries	Agricultural Products	Industrial Products	Total all Products
Low income countries			
Africa			
Central African Rep. (1)	10.8	9.9	10.1
Chad (1)	11.5	11.3	11.4
Malawi (2)	12.9	11.2	11.0
Tanzania (4)	33.8	22.4	23.7
Uganda (2)	30.9	23.5	24.3
Zaire	9.3	6.1	6.5
Asia			
Bangladesh (2)	64.4	78.1	76.0
India (1)	82.0	70.0	72.0
Pakistan (2)	79.4	73.2	74.0
Sri Lanka (2)	58.6	35.5	38.8
Middle income countries			
Africa			
Egypt (2)	45.3	38.9	40.6
Ghana (2)	33.6	34.6	34.4
Ivory Coast (2)	8.8	6.9	7.3
Liberia (3)	20.5	28.8	27.7
Mauritius (4)	10.1	14.7	14.4
Morocco (4)	44.5	27.8	30.7
Nigeria (3)	36.6	31.2	31.9
Tunisia (3)	27.1	16.1	18.2
Asia			
Korea** (1)	40.2	28.7	29.9
Iran* (2)	24.0	22.1	22.3
Philippines (2)	66.6	39.7	43.8
Latin America			
Argentina** (4)	14.6	30.3	27.0
Brazil** (2)	48.3	39.1	40.3
Bahamas (2)	26.8	30.8	30.1
Bolivia (2)	15.2	15.1	15.1
Chile (2)	15.4	23.7	22.6
Columbia (2)	27.8	28.0	28.0
Ecuador*	65.4	26.4	31.7
Jamaica (1)	16.8	16.3	16.4
Mexico** (4)	30.4	21.7	22.3
Paraquay (3)	9.8	11.4	11.1
Panama	12.1	14.3	14.1
Peru (2)	25.0	41.8	40.1
Suriname	28.5	23.6	24.5
Venezuela* (2)	85.0	35.2	41.9

Source: GATT, "Expansion of Trade Among Developing Countries" -- Technical Studies 1978-1979.

Note: Tariff rates are the unweighted arithmetic average of tariff lines by country compiled by GATT.

  *   OPEC Members.

**   Newly Industrialised Countries.

1.   1976 data.

2.   1977 data.

3.   1978 data.

4.   1979 data.

Table 3.8

AVERAGE DUTY RATES IN DEVELOPING COUNTRIES FOR AGRICULTURAL PRODUCTS (1)

(per cent)

Description (SITC Codes) (2)	Low Income Countries			Middle Income Countries			
	Africa (3)	Asia (4)	Total	Africa (5)	Asia (6)	Latin America (7)	Total
LIVE ANIMALS, MEAT AND MEAT PREPARATIONS							
Live animals, (001;941/01.01-06)	4.0	38.2	21.1	9.5	19.7	14.9	14.7
Meat, fresh, chilled or frozen (011/02.01-04)	14.2	114.1	64.2	28.1	29.1	18.3	25.2
Meat, dried, salted or smoked, meat preparations (012;013/02.06;16.01-03)	23.1	103.5	63.3	35.6	71.3	39.5	48.8
DAIRY PRODUCTS AND EGGS (022,023,024,025/04.01-05.04.07)	13.4	47.2	30.3	18.2	38.0	29.6	28.6
CEREALS AND CEREAL PREPARATIONS							
Cereals (041-045/10.01-07)	11.4	3.0	7.2	15.5	20.4	18.8	18.2
Meals and flours (046-047/11.01-02)	23.8	32.8	28.3	26.3	30.0	28.0	28.1
Cereal preparations (048;599.51-52/11.07-09; 19.01-03;19.05-08)	22.2	69.2	45.7	26.8	51.8	30.9	36.5
FRUIT AND VEGETABLES							
Vegetables, fresh, frozen or simply preserved (054/07.01-03;07.05-06;12.04-06;12.08)	20.2	83.7	52.0	24.4	35.7	20.3	26.8
Fruit and nuts, fresh and dried or temporarily preserved (051-052+053.6/08.01-0813;20.03)	25.0	83.8	54.4	33.7	58.5	27.3	39.8
Vegetables, roots, etc., preserved or prepared (055/07.04;11.03-06;19.04;20.01-02)	26.1	82.4	54.3	36.2	51.8	34.8	40.9
Fruit preserved and fruit preparations [053(excl. 053.6)/20.04-07]	27.8	127.5	77.7	53.0	69.1	52.8	58.3
SUGAR, SUGAR PREPARATIONS AND HONEY (061-062/17.01-05;04.06)	24.9	77.5	51.2	33.8	49.6	38.0	40.5
COCOA AND COCOA PRODUCTS							
Cocoa beans (072.1/18.01)	19.2	102.5	60.9	10.8	34.0	39.4	28.1
Cocoa butter and cocoa paste (072.3;073/18.03-04)	20.8	110.0	65.4	15.9	59.2	38.6	37.9
Cocoa powder and chocolate (072.2;073/18.05-06)	24.8	113.4	69.1	49.9	71.7	57.1	59.6
COFFEE, TEA, MATE							
Raw coffee (071.1/09.01)	20.2	125.0	72.6	36.1	66.7	24.7	42.5
Tea and maté (074/09.02;09.03)	22.5	(60.0) (8)	(41.3)	24.4	68.8	28.2	40.5
Coffee and tea extracts (071.3/21.02)	30.0	133.8	81.9	56.3	80.0	34.1	56.8
OILSEEDS, OILS AND FATS, ANIMAL FEEDING STUFFS							
Oilseeds (221/12.01-12.02)	16.0	61.6	38.8	14.2	31.3	21.7	22.4
Animal and vegetable oils and fats and waxes (091;411;421;422;431+512.25,512.26/02.05;15.01-17)	13.4	52.5	33.0	20.2	35.4	30.5	28.7
Feeding-stuff for animals (081/12.09-10;23.01-07;18.02)	10.4	42.9	26.7	12.2	21.1	14.9	16.1
AGRICULTURAL RAW MATERIALS (291-292;262.51/06.01-04;12.03;12.07;13.01-03; 14.01-05;05.01-05.15)	10.1	53.3	31.7	18.6	40.4	17.3	25.4
TOTAL "AGRICULTURAL PRODUCTS" (CCCN Chapter 1-24)	18.2	71.1	44.7	28.3	43.6	30.1	34.0

1. Unweighted arithmetic average.
2. Customs Co-operation Council Nomenclature.
3. Central African Republic Chad, Malawi, Tanzania, Uganda, Zaire.
4. Bangladesh, India, Pakistan, Sri Lanka.
5. Egypt, Ghana, Ivory Coast, Liberia, Mauritius, Morocco, Nigeria, Tunisia.
6. Iran, Korea, Philippines.
7. Argentina, Bahamas, Bolivia, Brazil, Chile, Colombia, Ecuador, Jamaica, Mexico, Panama, Paraguay, Peru, Surinam, Venezuela.
8. Bangladesh n.a.

Source: GATT, "Expansion of Trade Among Developing Countries" -- Technical Studies 1978-1979.

3.63. A breakdown of the tariff rates on agricultural products by major SITC code for LDCs is given in Table 3.8. It shows that tariff escalation with the level of processing is as evident in LDCs as it is in OECD countries. It also appears that the level of protection on LDC products – i.e. sugar, cocoa, coffee and tea – are higher than the level of protection on products coming primarily from OECD sources (dairy products, cereals, oilseeds and animal feeds). If this pattern is indicative of trade restrictions for all LDCs, it is clear that LDC tariffs are at least as great an impediment to increased exports of these major LDC products as OECD tariffs.

3.64. A policy area of growing significance for OECD exporters is the LDCs' approach towards livestock production. The growth of per capita incomes and the associated increase in demand for meat and livestock products confronts decision-makers in a number of LDCs with two possible, but not mutually exclusive, approaches: to develop a domestic livestock industry and import the necessary animal feeds or to import the livestock products directly. The path taken will depend on the particular situation in each country, but the overall trade impact of the policy approaches adopted by individual countries (e.g. the difference in the degree of protection provided grains versus meat and dairy products) will become more significant as more countries become more affluent and expand their demand for livestock products.

3.65. The theoretical choice available to the developing countries of whether or not to develop a livestock industry would have very important implications for OECD exporters. The growth of large scale domestic livestock industries in developing countries would favour grain producers in the major grain exporting countries such as the U.S., Canada, Australia and France. On the other hand, greater emphasis on imports of consumer products will favour dairy and livestock producers in the OECD countries which export these products. New Zealand, the Netherlands, Ireland, the United States, Australia and Denmark could benefit most from this approach.

3.66. Table 3.8 provides evidence that most developing countries having the possibility to develop a livestock industry have chosen this option rather than import livestock products. Ad valorem tariffs on cereals, oilseeds and feedstuffs are well below the rates for meats (excluding live animals) and are generally below the rates for dairy products. As more and more LDCs reach the level of development attained by South Korea, Taiwan and Hong Kong, these priorities will have a growing impact on the structure of world agricultural markets.

3.67. The policies of some of the NICs, in particular, are likely to affect the stability of world feedgrain prices. South Korea and Taiwan, for example, have established stabilisation funds for feedgrain imports. Both countries set an expected price for feedgrains each year. If actual prices exceed the expected price, payments to make up the difference are made out of a general fund to importers of the grains. If the actual price is less than the expected price, importers pay a tax equal to the difference in the two prices into the fund. This policy stabilizes prices to importers but, in doing so, prevents short-run adjustment in these countries to world price fluctuations. Because they are large and growing markets for feedgrains, the failure of these countries to adjust will increase the adjustments required for the rest of the world's feedgrain traders.

b) *Impact on OECD Importers*

3.68. LDC policies affect OECD countries through their impact on the level and stability of world prices. As noted earlier, world prices are strengthened by additional LDC imports resulting from pricing policies which subsidise domestic food consumption and discourage agricultural production. Many LDC export policies also have much the same effect. Agricultural exports are often taxed as a means of raising government revenue.

3.69. An indication of the rate at which exports are taxed in some LDCs is provided using the "Nominal Protection Coefficient" (NPC) defined as the price paid to the producer divided by

Table 3.9

NOMINAL PROTECTION COEFFICIENTS (NPC) FOR SELECTED AFRICAN EXPORT CROPS

Crop/Country	NPC, 1976-80
Cocoa	
Cameroon	0.45
Ghana	0.40
Ivory Coast	0.38
Togo	0.25
Coffee	
Cameroon (Arabica)	0.60
Ivory Coast	0.36
Tanzania	0.59
Togo	0.23
Cotton	
Ivory Coast	1.05
Malawi	0.75
Mali	0.44
Sudan	0.60
Togo	0.79
Groundnuts	
Malawi	0.59
Mali	0.43
Senegal	0.66
Sudan	0.67
Zambia	0.71
Maize	
Kenya	1.33
Malawi	1.34
Zambia	0.78
Tobacco	
Malawi	0.28
Zambia	0.88

Source: World Bank Development Report 1982.

the price he would have received had he sold his crops at the world price minus transportation, marketing and processing costs. An NPC value below 1.0 indicates taxation; a value above 1.0 indicates subsidisation. NPCs are shown for important export commodities for a selected group of African countries in Table 3.9[44]. The values in the table indicate that in all of the countries given and for all of the products shown, exports are being taxed – some at very high rates (with the exceptions of maize exports from Kenya and Malawi). These taxes discourage

exports, decrease the size of the world market and put upward pressure on world prices.
3.70. Exchange rate policies, which are not taken into account in the calculation of the NPC, can have the same effect. Governments in LDCs through their control banks, operate exchange rate policies whose effect is to tax exports. They require that all transactions be carried out at an officially fixed rate which, in foreign currency units per domestic unit, is less than the rate which would prevail in the absence of controls. Exporters, therefore, earn less for their products in domestic currency than they would if they could get a "market" rate of exchange. Recently it has been estimated that up to 10 per cent of Argentina's 1982 soyabean crop has been sold on the black market in Brazil and Paraguay to avoid the using the official exchange rate. The effects of exchange controls and export taxes are difficult to assess but it is clear that agricultural sectors in developing countries will not reach their full potential as long as these measures are employed in a way which discriminates against agriculture.
3.71. LDCs also affect OECD importers through their impact on the stability of world market prices. The effect of severing the link between domestic and world agricultural markets on the varibility of world prices has already been discussed in relation to OECD trade policies. It is worth re-emphasising here, however, that many LDC policies – particularly the use of fixed internal prices and control of trade with state trading agencies – have the same effect. The growing importance of LDCs in world agricultural markets and the prevalence of state trading regimes in many of these countries would indicate that other things being equal world price variability is likely to increase.

B. Multilateral Policies and Actions

3.72. The economic and agricultural policies of individual countries are necessarily designed and implemented with national objectives in mind. However, OECD Member countries often have certain international policy objectives. These two sets of objectives cannot be achieved exclusively through the use of domestic policies. Multilateral initiatives and instruments are needed to enable countries to find joint solutions to problems which cannot be solved through unilateral actions. Some multilateral actions which have a direct bearing on OECD/LDC agricultural trade are considered below.

1. *Food Security*

3.73. Food security is a major preoccupation of many developing countries, especially the poorer LDCs and it has an important influence on the manner in which these countries approach agricultural trade. Food security has been defined as "...the problem of ensuring that populations have continuous access to adequate food supplies..."[45]. This access to adequate food supplies can be provided from either domestic or foreign sources and will depend largely on the resources – and to a lesser extent the policies – of the individual country.
3.74. Within the context of agricultural trade, food security concerns affect the approach taken towards food distribution in two different aspects. First, there is the provision for the physical distribution of food, i.e. the construction of adequate transportation, storage and marketing facilities to ensure that food supplies are delivered throughout the country on a timely basis. The level of the development of these facilities affects the size and timing of purchases or sales on world markets. Second there is the concern of distributing adequate food supplies to all members of the population regardless of income levels. (The "cheap food" policies in many LDCs are designed specifically to help the poorest groups of people to obtain a

minimum level of food intake.) These policies affect the types of foods consumed and, to a lesser extent, total caloric intake by the population.

3.75. The problem of food security can and must be addressed in many different ways by many different countries and involves both a long-term and a short-term dimension. Policies which address the long-term problem include such measures as investments in agriculture to improve productivity (as India has done successfully in the past 20 years); the provision of adequate price incentives to agricultural producers (as Cameroon has done); or investment in other sectors of the economy, such as textiles and light manufacturing, from which foreign exchange can be earned to purchase food imports (such as Taiwan, South Korea and Hong Kong have done). Policies which address the short-term dimension are concerned either with covering temporary shortfalls in production in domestic or world markets and the resulting price effects or with providing for food needs for a few years until the measures to address the longer term problem take effect.

3.76. The principal international fora for the discussion of the multilateral aspects of food security are the U.N. World Food Council; and the FAO Committee on World Food Security. The responsibility for concrete action and negotiation rests with the GATT for trade matters, the IMF for financial matters, the International Wheat Copuncil for wheat agreements and the Committee on Food Aid and Policies and for Programs for food aid questions and in particular the World Food Program. Most of the multilateral initiatives discussed below are those which are designed to address the short-term food security problem. The longer term aspects of food security are broader measures which include both domestic and international investments in the production capacity of a nation's economy.

3.77. There are three broad international approaches which have a bearing on the food security needs of LDCs. One is to provide either direct food aid or the funds with which to make food purchases to LDCs. A second longer term approach is to provide development assistance which will improve the ability of developing countries to meet their own food needs. A third approach is to stabilize or improve the export earnings of LDCs through technical assistance and other means so that they can continue to make essential import purchases of which food is often the most important. All three of these approaches have different implications for world agricultural markets and commercial agricultural trade.

a) *Food Aid and Food Finance Programmes*[46]

3.78 The OECD Member countries provide food aid to LDCs through a variety of bilateral and multilateral programmes. Total allocations of food aid for 1982/83 were 9.3 million tonnes (in grain equivalent) of which 97 per cent was cereals[47]. OECD Members contributed all but 1 per cent of the total. The United States and the EEC were the largest donors with contributions of 5.4 and 1.7 million tonnes respectively. The FAO *Principles of Surplus Disposal* play a role in regulating both the bilateral and the multilateral disbursement of food aid. These principles were "designed to ensure that the supply of food to developing countries as aid, or on concessional markets, did not disrupt or threaten to disrupt commercial markets"[48].

3.79. Although attempts are made to prevent food aid from disrupting commercial markets, food aid ultimately has some repercussions on these markets. Food aid may have a positive effect on indigenous transportation, storage and processing facilities thereby enhancing the infrastructure for commercial trade. The short-run effect is to reduce somewhat the quantities which are traded on commercial terms. The actual amount by which commercial sales are reduced is an empirical question and depends heavily on the assumptions made about the purchasing policies which would be pursued by recipient governments in the absence of food

aid and concessional sales. Most recipient governments would probably import smaller total quantities of food and probably also a smaller proportion of foods from OECD suppliers.
3.80. The long-run effects of food aid on commercial sales are not as obvious. Food aid may have actually increased commercial sales in the long-run by encouraging a change in tastes away from traditional tropical foods (e.g. cassava, sorghum, maize and rice) towards temperate foods – primarily wheat. Food aid, however, is only a contributing cause of this shift in consumption patterns since rising incomes, urbanisation and consumer subsidy policies in LDCs have also had a major influence. More balanced nutritional patterns in most cases result from the availability of both indigenous and temperate foods. Yet food aid has certainly hastened the speed with which this change in consumption patterns has taken place.
3.81. Food aid has increasingly (19 per cent in 1976, 36 per cent in 1981) been channelled through multilateral agencies notably the UN/FAO World Food Programme (WFP). This expansion partly reflects the experience and expertise of the WFP in undertaking projects that use food aid to meet humanitarian and development needs in a manner supportive both of local food production efforts and the trading system. Most of the cereals and financial resources of the WFP are provided by OECD countries. The value of net commitments of food aid to WFP in 1982 is estimated to be $576 million compared to $488 million in 1981. The pattern of expenditure in 1981 was of the order of 70 per cent for development projects and 25 per cent emergency operations.
3.82. Food aid does not necessarily have to be provided in kind. In some cases financial assistance is provided to LDCs to increase their purchasing power so that they can buy the quantities they need. For example, a recent international initiative to assist LDCs to cover the additional costs of an increase in world cereal prices is the IMF's Compensatory Financing Facility (sometimes referred to as the *Food Financing Facility*)[49]. This Facility was created in May 1981 and grew out of the comprehensive Plan of Action on World Food Security adopted by FAO in 1979 and the World Food Council Resolution. This Facility provides for compensation to be made available to members for excesses in the cost of cereal imports. Under the decision such compensation is integrated with that available for export short-falls. As of March 1983 this facility had been used five times by several developing countries for amounts totalling SDR 344 million. In essence, the Food facility has less of an impact on the long-term volume of trade than do concessional sales and/or food aid. Inasmuch as the Facility provides funds for the purchase of all cereals, it gives LDCs flexibility in their purchases and is less likely to encourage a change in LDC consumption patterns.

b) *Development Assistance*

3.83. Development assistance is an important element in food security considerations for developing countries because it addresses the longer term food needs of individual developing countries. In 1980 Member countries of the OECD Development Assistance Committee (DAC) committed $8.5 billion in *bilateral* development aid to low-income LDCs, of which $3.2 billion was destined for the poorest LDCs. Normally about one-half of this total is committed to improving agricultural production in these countries. For example, in 1979 aid to these countries for agricultural purposes amounted to $4.4 billion. Total aid commitments for agricultural purposes to all developing countries reached $7 billion, a 100 per cent increase over 1973 in constant prices.
3.84. Development finance provided by *multilateral* agencies in 1981 amounted to $13 billion (net disbursements). Over 60 per cent of this total ($8 billion) was on concessional terms. Multilateral agencies accounted for 24 per cent of developing countries' total ODA receipts, after a decade in which the multilateral share had risen steadily from 14 per cent in

1971. Contributions from DAC members in 1980-81 amounted to 25 per cent of total, down from 30 per cent in 1976-77. The major part of multilateral aid is disbursed through UN agencies, the World Bank, and the International Development Association. Certain aid programmes of the EEC are also important. It is difficult to isolate the agricultural aspects of multilateral aid. However, agriculture plays a very important role. Perhaps as much as one half could be ascribed to agricultural development[50].

3.85. The effects of development assistance on trade volumes and flows is extremely difficult to quantify in aggregate terms. However, it is obvious that certain individual projects can have a significant impact on trade. For example, the successes of the green revolution in Asia have decreased the need for imported grains into this region. On the other hand the development of grain-based livestock sub-sectors in some developing countries (especially the NICs) has created a greater dependance on imported cereals. In general, development programmes which promote self-sufficiency, decrease the need for food imports, while other programmes may stimulate the production of export-oriented crops. In either case such programmes are likely to affect both the volume and/or flow of trade over the long-term.

2. *Export earnings stability*

3.86. Stability of export earnings for developing countries can be an important element in the overall export performance of the developing countries. It is of particular concern for those countries which are dependent on a single commodity or a small number of commodities for the majority of their foreign exchange. Three major factors contribute to instability of these earnings: (*a*) the inherent instability of agricultural markets; (*b*) fluctuations in the export performance of an individual country (changes in production, government policies, problems relating to infrastructure, etc.); and, (*c*) the ability of importing countries to purchase such commodities at remunerative prices to LDC producers. The following paragraphs discuss selected multilateral initiatives which have addressed the problem of stabilizing the export earnings of the developing countries.

a) *International Commodity Agreements and Arrangements*

3.87. The concept of international agreements to improve the conditions of commodity trade, notably by stabilising price levels, was pioneered by the Havana Charter of 1948, part of which was absorbed into the GATT Articles. The principal objectives of stabilization agreements have normally been to achieve a more stable equilibrium between supply and demand for commodities traditionally subject to considerable fluctuations in both, and to stabilize prices at levels which will be remunerative to producers and equitable to consumers without losing touch with long-term market trends; additional objectives normally include development considerations. The mechanisms usually employed have principally been buffer stocks and/or supply management by production or export quotas. The results achieved in practice have been variable due to a variety of factors and reasons which vary according to the commodity and type of agreement or arrangement. Hence, generalisations concerning these market mechanisms are difficult. "Each commodity agreement represents many different hopes and aspirations for many different countries. The question whether it is feasible to develop one instrument which will achieve such a far-reaching range of objectives or even a more limited objective such as containing prices within a given range, is essentially one to be determined by each commodity's producers and consumers. These have, first, to determine whether there is a need for a stabilisation agreement and next to choose, among a range of measures including buffer stocks and supply management techniques such as export quotas, which measure or combination of measures is appropriate and likely to be effective. Account must also be taken of the sometimes daunting range of technical complications involved in allowing for types and grades of product according to quality, use, value and market. All these factors often involve conflicting interests as well as the difficulties in obtaining the participation of all major producing and consuming countries and it is not therefore surprising that stabilization agreements are difficult to conclude, and do not always achieve the desired improvements in the functioning of world markets in the products concerned"[51].

3.88. The principal focus of international co-operation in the commodities field has been the UNCTAD, in particular two major consensus resolutions adopted, one by the 1976 Conference initiating the *Integrated Programme for Commodities,* including the *Common Fund* – Resolution 93(IV), and the other the 1979 Conference resolution following up the Integrated Programme but also embodying "developmental aspects" of commodity policy – Resolution 124(V); at the latter Conference another text on export earnings stabilisation – Resolution 125(V) – was adopted by majority vote only. From these fundamental texts four strands of international co-operation can be distinguished:

  a) *price stabilization* through international agreements, particularly those involving buffer stocks and thus able to make use of the first window of the Common Fund;
  b) *"other measures"* envisaged in the Integrated Programme which will be able to make use of the second window of the Common Fund – i.e. commodity-specific rather than country-specific measures – to attain its objectives;
  c) the *"developmental measures"* spelled out in Resolution 124(V), principally those aiming at increased participation of developing countries in the processing and in the marketing and distribution of the commodities they produce;
  d) improvements in systems of *compensatory financing* for shortfalls in export earnings from commodities, to which (majority) resolution 125(V) was relevant.

3.89. Though price stabilization was only one of the agreed objectives, it was probably inevitable that it assumed particular importance in the elaboration of the Integrated Programme, partly because it was spelled out in more detail than others – as also were the appropriate measures – and partly because of the proposals for the Common Fund which was accepted generally as a key element in the programme. Though this prominence has been maintained, the fact that it was only one of several objectives has been reflected in subsequent developments. In particular, pressure from the developing countries, particularly in Africa where little benefit was foreseen for them in the assistance which buffer stock financing would offer, ensured that the Fund would have a *second window* to finance other measures. Consequently, a new breed of international commodity body has emerged, for example the recent arrangement concerning jute.

3.90. Of five commodities for which international stabilization agreements have been concluded, only three – rubber, cocoa and tin – provide for international buffer stocks: the sugar agreement provides for nationally held stocks, (see Table 3.10). There are a number of other underlying problems: incomplete membership (sugar, cocoa, tin): producer/consumer differences, mainly on stock acquisition and release prices; differences between producers, mainly on quota allocation. A number of problems will have to be resolved before these agreements would associate with the fund.

3.91. As regards agricultural commodities and the second window, there has been more substantial progress, which has required elaboration of a new type of commodity body, although some problems are unresolved. For vegetable oils and oilseeds, meat and bananas, projects have been defined and further action handed over to the FAO groups involved. Discussions concerning jute resulted in a formal arrangement in late 1982 and discussions

Table 3.10

PRINCIPAL FEATURES OF INTERNATIONAL AGRICULTURAL COMMODITY AGREEMENTS AND SELECTED COMMODITY ARRANGEMENTS (1)

Commodity	Entry into force	Target prices	Export or prod.quotas	Buffer stocks
Formal Agreements				
Sugar (2)	1978	yes	yes	yes (3)
Coffee	1976	yes	yes	no
Cocoa (4)	1980	yes	no	yes
Olive oil	1980	no	no	no
Natural rubber	1980	yes	no	yes
Formal Arrangements				
Bovine meat	1980	no	no	no
Dairy products	1980	yes, min export	no	no
Jute, Kenaf and allied fibres	1982	no	no	no
Informal Arrangements				
Tea	1970	no	yes	no
Abaca	1968	yes	no	no
Sisal and Henequen	1967	yes	yes (6)	no
Convention				
Wheat (5)	1971	no	no	no

1. Adapated from **Commodity Review and Outlook** reports, FAO, 1980-81 and 1981-82. Unless otherwise stated major producer and consumer countries participate in each respective Agreement.

2. The EEC, a major sugar producer and consumer, does not participate.

3. Nationally held stocks.

4. The Ivory Coast as a major producer and the USA as a major consumer do not participate.

5. The Food Aid Convention entered into force on 1 July 1980.

6. Currently suspended.

involving tropical timber, hard fibres and bananas are at an advanced stage. It is likely that some of these agreements such as bananas will make use of the second window.

b) *IMF: Compensatory Financing Facility*

3.92. The Compensatory Financing Facility (CFF), which was established in 1963, provides support to IMF members experiencing balance of payments difficulties arising from temporary shortfalls in export receipts largely attributable to circumstances beyond a member's control. Repurchases of a member's currency under the facility are made on the same three to five year conditions as repurchases under the normal credit tranches. Following liberalisation of the IMF facility in 1975 and 1979, drawings outstanding may now amount to 100 per cent of a member's quota in the Fund, there is no limitation on the amount which can be drawn in any twelve month period and earnings from services can be included in the calculation of shortfall. According to Fund staff estimates, as a result of the 1979 liberalisation the coverage rate of compensation has now reached more than two-thirds of shortfalls (compared with one-half achieved under th 1975 decision). Purchases under the CFF between 1975 and January 1983 amounted to some SDR 6 160 million. Purchases in 1982 were SDR 2 628 million, more than double the 1981 level. At the end of 1982 outstanding purchases amounted to SDR 5 398 million[52].

c) *EEC: The STABEX Scheme*

3.93. In 1979 the Lomé II Convention signed by the EEC members and 62 ACP states renewed its STABEX system of export earnings stabilization for the 1981-85 period. This system compensates for shortfalls in earnings from agricultural commodity exports from the ACP states to the EEC. The scheme covers 44 commodities, including almost all agricultural products exported to a significant degree to the EEC and a few processed commodities.

3.94. Membership in the STABEX scheme is possible for the 47 poorest developing ACP states if their exports to the EEC account for at least 2 per cent of their total exports of the commodity in question. This "dependence" level is 6.5 per cent for other ACP members. Similarly, compensation for losses in export receipts is triggered only after these receipts fall by the above percentages (based on a reference period of the previous four years). The poorest developing countries receive compensation in the form of grants: interest-free loans are available to the others. Loans can be repaid over five years with a two-year grace period.

3.95. The IMF Compensatory Financing Facility described above differs from STABEX in its global nature and the fact that it covers total export earnings and thus compensates on net shortfalls rather than on gross shortfalls in commodity earnings; charges are at the same rate as for other general resources accounts and are thus less concessionary than in STABEX; and, in calculating shortfalls, the scheme incorporates a two-year forecast of exports (in addition to using data for the current year and two previous years).

3.96. Under the previous Lomé I Agreement (1974-79) period 123 STABEX transfers were made, for a total of about EUA 375 million. Benin, Mauritania, Niger, Senegal and Sudan accounted for 50 per cent of these STABEX transactions: morethan 50 per cent of all transfers were for agricultural commodities. Resources allocated for the 1981-84 STABEX system are EUA 550 million for agricultural commodities only[53].

d) *IMF: Buffer Stock Facility*

3.97. Fund assistance is available to members in balance of payments difficulties for the purpose of financing their contributions to buffer stocks of primary products established under international commodity agreements that are judged to be suitable for Fund financing. In accordance with criteria laid down in the decision establishing the facility, the Fund has so far authorised the use of its resources in connection with the tin, and sugar buffer stocks, and purchases have been made only with respect to these commodities. Six members have purchased a total of about SDR 30 million in connection with their contributions to the buffer stock established under the Fourth International Tin Agreement, and six members have utilised about SDR 74 million for contributions under the International Sugar Agreement. All of these purchases have been repaid. In late 1982 the Facility was expanded to include buffer stocks of rubber.

e) *The Arab Monetary Fund*

3.98. This Fund, set up in 1971 with 21 members, assists member states in balance-of-payments difficulties resulting from a decrease in receipts from exports of goods and services or a large increase in imports of agricultural products following a poor harvest. Loans, extended for amounts up to 100 per cent of a member's paid-up capital are intended to complement IMF CFF drawings and are repayable within three years. The first loan was extended to Sudan ($20 million) in 1979/80 to compensate for a poor cotton harvest.

f) *General Aspects of Export Earnings Stability Schemes*

3.99. Export earnings stability is desirable for both LDCs and their trading partners. For LDCs the assurance of a measure of export earnings stability allows them to make long term resource commitments for export production at a lower level of risk. Trading partners benefit because more stable LDC export earnings should translate into more stable import purchases. There is an advantage to directly addressing the question of earnings stability of individual countries through financing (e.g., the CCF and STABEX) rather than through commodity agreements. International commodity agreements are relatively blunt instruments and are not easily targeted to the problems of individual countries. They are also difficult to define, implement and operate and they may create market distortions. Compensatory financing arrangements have a neutral effect on price formation. Certainly more targeted assistance is possible through financing schemes and this would seem desirable. It is clear that commodity problems, as they affect LDCs, is an area of significant concern for both LDCs themselves and their trading partners.

3. *Export Expansion*

3.100. Export expansion schemes between OECD and the developing countries have taken many forms over the years. Such schemes are basically designed to promote the expansion of exports from the LDCs; some of the foreign exchange revenues resulting from increased exports will be used to increase imports from the OECD countries. Hence the interdependency aspect of expanded trade is an important aspect of these schemes. The following section describes important multilateral efforts to expand exports from the developing countries. i.e. the GATT, the generalised scheme of preferences, the Lomé Convention and other selected schemes.

a) *The GATT: Its Relationship to the Developing Countries*

3.101. The developing countries have been involved in GATT since its inception, when they comprised 10 of the original 23 founding countries. Currently about two-thirds of the 89

Member countries of GATT are developing countries, and they look to the GATT as a vehicle to promote the expansion of their trade and thus to contribute to their economic development, with due regard for their special circumstances and needs. From the beginning, Article XVIII released the LDCs from certain obligations of membership and in 1965, other Articles under Part IV were added concerning the special situation of developing countries, e.g. they would not be expected in the course of trade negotiations, to make contributions inconsistent with their individual development, financial and trade needs. At the same time a Committee on Trade and Development was set up to monitor GATT activities under Part IV and to ensure that problems concerning developing countries are given priority attention.

3.102. The Tokyo Round of negotiations stressed the position of the developing countries and several paragraphs of the Tokyo Declaration were devoted to the LDCs and specifically to the poorest LDCs. For example, the Declaration re-iterated the concept of non-reciprocity, by stating "The developed countries do not expect reciprocity for commitments made by them in the negotiations to reduce or remove tariff and other barriers to the trade of developing countries, i.e. the developed countries do not expect the developing countries... to make contributions which are inconsistent with their individual development, financial and trade needs"[54]. In general the concept of the non-reciprocity is sometimes applied somewhat selectively by the OECD countries. Nevertheless, developing countries benefitted from a number of reductions in trade barriers facing their exports in the Tokyo Round, as well as more flexible provisions in their implementation of Tokyo Round agreements covering tariffs, NTBs, and tropical products. Another major result of the Tokyo Round was the adoption of the "enabling clause" in the form of a decision opening the way to recognition of tariff and non-tariff preferential treatment in favour of and between developing countries as a continuing feature of the world trading system. This provided inter alia a more explicit basis for the generalised system of preferences, originally authorised by a temporary waiver of the most-favoured-nation provisions of the GATT.

3.103. The specific implications of the Tokyo Round negotiations for the developing countries' agricultural exports are complex and difficult to quantify adequately. However, certain results regarding tariffs and NTBs were obtained for agriculture. A source of tariff reductions agreed in the Tokyo Round began on 1 January 1980 and will continue with equal annual cuts, the total reduction to become effective not later than 1 January 1987. The total value of trade affected by Tokyo Round most-favoured-nation (MFN) tariff reductions, and by bindings of prevailing tariff rates is more than $155 billion (measured in 1977 MFN imports). Developing countries made tariff reductions on $3.9 billion of their imports in 1977[55]. As regards agricultural products and the LDCs, the rates of reduction were less than for industrial products. For example, for agricultural products as a whole the post-MTN tariffs were 12 per cent (weighted average) and 7 per cent (simple average) below their pre-MTN levels, compared to corresponding percentages of 26 per cent and 37 per cent, respectively for all industrial products[56]. Reductions in import duties and other barriers to trade facing LDCs exports of *tropical* products were the first concrete results of the MTN: most were implemented in 1976 and 1977 and in 1980. Products such as coffee, cocoa, tea, spices and a variety of other goods in raw, processed and semi-processed forms were also covered to varying extents.

3.104. As regards *non-tariff measures* for agricultural products the greatest progress was apparent in the Arrangements regarding bovine meat and dairy products. Even according to UNCTAD, which was generally critical of the results of the MTN, the results of the negotiations concerning meat (the Bovine Meat Arrangement) were of "modest value" and the International Dairy Arrangement "could help to meet some of the concerns of the developing countries with regard to trade in dairy products"[57]. As for agriculture as a whole

UNCTAD's assessment was generally positive: "it appears that for agricultural products, supplies from developing countries would benefit from increased MFN duty-free admission and increased GSP coverage"[58].

3.105. More recently trade in agriculture was highlighted in the GATT Ministerial Declaration. Although the developing countries were not mentioned specifically in this part of the Declaration it emphasised the "urgent need to find lasting solutions to the problems of trade in agricultural products". It was agreed that the contracting parties would conduct an examination of national agricultural policies which "affect trade, market access and competition and supply in agricultural products, including subsidies and other forms of assistance". A plan of action was outlined whereby an agricultural trade committee would be established, open to all contracting parties to carry out these tasks. More important for the LDCs the Declaration committed contracting parties to further work on consultations and appropriate negotiations aimed at "further liberalisation of trade in tropical products, including their processed and semi-processed forms, and to review progress achieved in eliminating or reducing existing obstacles to trade in tropical products..."[59].

  b) *Preferential Trading Arrangements affecting the Developing Countries*

   i) The Generalised System of Preferences[60]

3.106. The concept of the GSP was first considered at the 1964 UNCTAD I Conference and accepted at the 1968 UNCTAD II Conference. This scheme is most relevant to manufactured and/or semi-processed LDC exports. The objectives include non-reciprocal, non-discriminatory preferences toward developing countries including special measures concerning the poorest LDCs. The GSP goals are to promote industrialisation, increase export earnings and to accelerate rates of growth in developing countries. One of the most important aspects of the GSP is that preferential access is on a non-reciprocal basis; however, access is often circumscribed by product exclusion and by limitations on the preferences granted.

3.107. Twenty OECD countries have provisions which grant GSP concessions to the developing countries. Most schemes have a restricted coverage of agricultural products and also grant limited preferences to products such as textiles, clothing and footwear.

3.108. Table 3.11 gives an indication of the evolution of total North-South trade flows in the period since the GSP was implemented. The most direct indication is the fact that during the 1970s the amount of trade imported under the GSP into OECD preference-giving countries grew strikingly. From about $1 billion in 1972 (the first complete year of operation for the earliest schemes), preferential trade rose to $4.5 billion by 1975. The following year, with the implementation of the United States scheme, total GSP imports jumped to over $10 billion. Rapid growth continued over the rest of the decade bringing the figure to about $25.4 billion for the eleven individual OECD schemes in 1980.

3.109. The evolution of imports under the GSP should be viewed in the context of broader trends in international trade. During the 1970s, *total imports* of preference-giving countries from beneficiary countries were also growing, although generally at a slower rate than the portion of these imports which benefitted from the GSP. Thus, for the latter part of the decade (1976-1980) the average annual growth rate of GSP imports approached 27 per cent, compared to about 20 per cent for total imports from beneficiaries. Apart from fuels, the product category which was the most dynamic in OECD imports for developing countries was manufactures, which was also the category the most completely covered by the GSP. During this period, OECD imports of manufactures from developing countries thus grew at an average annual rate of 23.4 per cent, while imports of these products from all sources grew at 18.8 per cent per year.

Table 3.11

OECD PREFERENCE-GIVING COUNTRIES' IMPORTS FROM
BENEFICIARY COUNTRIES: OVERVIEW 1972-1980 (*)

(Billions of US dollars)

	Total	Total dutiable	Covered by GSP	Accorded GSP treatment
1972	35.0	15.9	4.3	1.0
1973	43.2	24.0	6.6	2.2
1974	102.1	44.6	12.4	4.2
1975	100.7	43.9	12.0	4.5
1976	146.4	74.0	23.7	10.2
1977	160.7	82.4	26.8	12.4
1978	167.4	89.5	33.5	15.0
1979	224.5	124.0	42.4	20.3
1980	308.8	178.7	55.4	25.4

*) The figures in this table represent totals for those OECD preference-giving countries with operating GSP schemes in each given year. The following countries are included beginning in the years indicated:

1972: EEC, Japan, Austria, Finland, Norway, Sweden, Switzerland, UK.
1975: Australia, Canada.
1976: USA, New Zealand.

The contributions of Australia, Japan and New Zealand to the figures in this table are calendar year estimates.

Source: OECD.

3.110. Table 3.12, adapted from a recent OECD study[61] provides details of agricultural, industrial and total GSP imports by selected countries from all beneficiary countries. Breakdowns concerning agricultural and industrial imports are not always possible for certain countries due to their national accounting procedures. As the Table shows (column f) imports accorded GSP treatment as a percentage of dutiable imports reached almost 50 per cent in Sweden in 1980: percentage for other countries (where available) varied between 13 and 20 per cent. Column g is perhaps more revealing, as it demonstrates that about three-fourths of the agricultural imports covered by the GSP (for most countries) are accorded GSP treatment: (the percentage for the EEC is 57 per cent). In all cases in column f the percentage for agricultural imports under the GSP are greater than the percentages applicable to industrial products.

Table 3.12

GSP: OECD PREFERENCE-GIVING COUNTRIES' IMPORTS FROM BENEFICIARY COUNTRIES, 1976 AND 1980

Preference-giving country			Value in millions of US dollars				Percentages		
			Imports from Beneficiary Countries				Imports covered as % of dutiable imports C/B	Imports accorded GSP as % of dutiable imports D/B	Utilisation rate D/C
			Total	Dutiable (1)	Covered by GSP (2)	Accorded GSP treatment			
			(A)	(B)	(C)	(C)	(E)	(F)	(G)
AUSTRIA	1976 :	ag.	313.9	139.6	62.5	7.5	44.8	5.4	12.0
		ind.	1 017.8	868.7	820.3	116.8	94.4	13.4	14.2
		total	1 331.7	1 008.3	882.8	124.3	87.6	12.3	14.1
	1980 :	ag.	561.4	208.0	51.9	38.6	25.0	18.6	74.4
		ind.	2 582.1	554.7	471.1	308.2	84.9	55.6	65.4
		total	3 143.5	762.7	523.0	346.8	68.6	45.4	66.3
FINLAND	1976 :	ag.	293.6	106.3	7.4	4.9	7.0	4.6	66.2
		ind.	453.6	39.3	21.9	15.9	55.7	40.5	72.6
		total	747.2	145.7	29.3	20.8	20.1	14.3	71.0
	1980 :	ag.	509.1	171.0	37.9	27.8	22.2	16.3	73.4
		ind.	1 525.8	148.0	78.3	56.9	52.9	38.4	72.7
		total	2 035.0	319.0	116.3	84.8	36.5	26.6	72.9
JAPAN (*)	FY 1976-1977 :	ag.	4 031.1	3 051.6	391.5	366.2	12.8	12.0	93.5
		ind.	32 594.6	26 485.6	3 059.3	1 423.4	11.6	5.4	46.5
		total	36 625.8	29 537.1	3 450.8	1 789.5	11.7	6.1	51.9
	1980-81 :	ag.	6 236.6	4 635.3	977.1	901.6	21.1	19.5	92.3
		ind.	81 882.8	66 993.5	7 509.7	4 083.0	11.2	6.1	54.4
		total	88 119.4	71 628.8	8 486.8	4 984.6	11.8	7.0	58.7
SWEDEN	1976 :	ag.	555.8	356.4	31.2	27.3	6.8	7.7	87.5
		ind.	2 076.0	453.7	148.0	109.9	32.6	24.2	74.3
		total	2 631.8	810.1	179.1	137.2	32.1	16.9	76.6
	1980 :	ag.	774.2	83.4	50.2	41.0	60.2	49.1	81.7
		ind.	4 948.9	895.1	417.7	292.1	46.7	32.6	69.9
		total	5 723.1	978.6	467.9	333.1	47.8	34.0	71.2
SWITZERLAND	1976 :	ag.	499.8	409.8	36.3	26.2	8.9	6.4	72.2
		ind.	1 124.5	1 091.3	598.4	230.7	54.8	21.1	38.6
		total	1 624.3	1 501.1	634.7	256.9	42.3	17.1	40.5
	1980 :	ag.	877.1	765.9	129.1	100.8	16.9	13.2	78.1
		ind.	3 090.6	3 034.5	1 738.6	574.8	57.3	18.9	33.1
		total	3 967.8	3 800.4	1 867.6	675.7	49.1	17.8	36.2
UNITED STATES	1976 :	ag.	7 161.2		1 587.6	560.4			35.3
		ind.	21 336.4		4 942.4	2 599.9			52.6
		total	28 497.6	21 879.8	6 530.0	3 160.3	34.9	16.9	48.4
	1980 :	ag.							
		ind.							
		total	73 346.4	57 543.4	14 337.8	7 319.6	24.9	12.7	51.1
EEC (3)	1976 :	ag.	8 862.0	6 908.7	1 039.1	847.4	15.0	12.3	81.6
		ind.	58 986.7	11 041.3	9 863.9	3 066.8	89.3	27.8	31.1
		total	67 848.7	17 950.0	10 903.0	3 914.2	60.7	21.8	35.9
	1980 :	ag.	13 773.5		3 288.2	7 880.3			
		ind.	104 344.6		23 421.9	7 461.0			
		total	118 118.2	37 891.4	26 710.1	9 341.3	70.5	24.7	35.0

*) FY = Fiscal year. For Japan begins on 1st April.

1. i.e., imports which are dutiable before the application of the GSP. Imports admitted under temporary duty suspensions on a non-discriminatory basis are considered to be duty-free and are thus not included in columns 3, 4 or 5. (This is of importance particularly for figures relating to Austria and Norway.)

2. i.e. dutiable imports of products normally eligible for the GSP. In general, preferential limits are not taken into account in this column, nor are products eligible for other preferential arrangements, including handicraft arrangements.

3. Developing countries benefiting from preferential arrangements with the EEC other than the GSP are counted only in column 1. However, Yugoslavia has been counted in all columns.

Note: Product categories: Agriculture (Ag.) = CCN Chapters 1-24 (SITC: 0+1+22+29+4+971); Industry (Ind.) = CCCN Chapters 25-99; CCCN = Customs Co-operation Council Nomenclature.

Source: OECD, The Generalised System of Preferences: Review of the First Decade, Paris 1983, pp. 82-83.

3.111. The GSP has been more widely used by a small number of more advanced LDCs (primarily the NICs, plus India, China and Yugoslavia) reflecting their greater capability for taking advantage of the schemes. Concerning the need to request preferential treatment, many developing country exporters may not be aware of the GSP or may not have accurate information about its coverage and how it operates, despite the efforts made by various donor countries and international organisations to inform them and officials in their countries of the opportunities available. As a recent study concluded, "the low levels of utilisation by the poorest LDCs highlight the need for some beneficiary countries to improve their supply response, and for complementary measures to help them in doing so"[62]. It is likewise necessary for traders to find sufficient interest in obtaining preferential benefits that they carry out the required procedures. For several schemes, the failure of nominal beneficiaries to fulfil the preliminary notification requirements remains a significant factor in limiting actual GSP imports. In addition, in the case of products subject to very low MFN duties, or where the preferential margin is small, there may not be a large incentive to request GSP treatment[63].

ii) EEC: Lomé Convention

3.112. The Lomé Convention, which was originally signed in 1975 and renegotiated in 1980 for a further five years, was preceded by the Yaoundé Convention, originally concluded in 1963 and covering at that time 18 African developing countries. At present 63 countries of Africa, the Caribbean and the Pacific (ACP countries, 21 of which are on the United Nations list of least developed countries) benefit from the Lomé Convention. In accordance with this Convention, the EEC provides duty-free entry without preferential limits to all products with the exception of a few agricultural products which enter at reduced rates of duty. The main exceptions are rice, maize, beef and fresh oranges. For some agricultural products, notably beef, rum, sugar and bananas, there are other concessions or special arrangements. In the case of a comparatively small number of agricultural products of ACP origin which face duties and levies on importation into the EEC, the import charges are usually less than those applicable to non-ACP goods and, in some cases, they are almost entirely waived. It is likewise noteworthy that rules of origin are somewhat more liberal than those applying under the GSP and in particular permit both donor country content and cumulation among ACP countries. The convention also contains provisions relating to aid and industrial, financial and technical co-operation. Stabilisation of export receipts is provided under the Stabex scheme to exporters of a certain number of commodities including several minerals (see para. 3.92).

3.113. The ACP countries are also nominal GSP beneficiaries; however, as more extensive benefits are generally available to them under the Lomé Convention, they have (for most products) an advantage in using the Lomé preference instead of the GSP. In 1980 EEC imports from the ACP countries that were eligible for preferential treatment under the GSP amounted to $7.5 billion.

iii) EEC: Other Special Trading Arrangements

3.114. The EEC also has cooperation agreements with the *Maghreb* (Algeria, Morocco and Tunisia) and the *Mashreq* (Egypt, Jordan, Syria and Lebanon) countries. These agreements are wide-ranging, covering trade, economic, industrial co-operation and financial aid. The preferential trade system is broad but accompanied by certain measures such as import calendars, safeguard clauses, etc. For agricultural exports under the Maghreb agreement, tariff concessions vary between 20-100 per cent covering 80-90 per cent of dutiable exports. It is also noteworthy that, as a temporary measure, these countries continue to enjoy special preferential access to the French market. The agricultural trade concessions for the Mashreq countries are somewhat more limited than those applying to the Maghreb. For processed agricultural products, the fixed element of the CAP charges levied on most products has been removed, but the variable import levy – that which compensates Community producers for fluctuations between world and EEC prices of inputs used – still remains. Roughly 80 per cent of dutiable agricultural imports from these countries benefit from tariff concessions of 40-80 per cent. The Mashreq agreements also include an aid package and substantial food aid is provided outside the terms of the agreements.

3.115. Although all the Maghreb and Mashreq countries are beneficiaries of the EEC's GSP, the treatment accorded under their individual agreements with the Community is more favourable in a number of respects, as described above. The seven countries are thus encouraged to export to the EEC under those agreements. In 1980, over $4 billion worth of imports from these countries were eligible for preferences under the agreements, representing one third of the Community's total imports from these countries and 96.3 per cent of its dutiable imports from them.

3.116. Other significant EEC agreements exist with countries such as Malta, Cyprus and Israel and with OECD Member countries such as Spain, Portugal and Turkey (with the latter country in the form of an association agreement), as well as with Yugoslavia. These agreements involve special concessions for agricultural exports from these countries to the EEC. Yugoslavia has been a major beneficiary of GSP preferences in its trade with the EEC.

iv) Caribbean Basin Initiative

3.117. The United States, in conjunction with Mexico, Canada and Venezuela, proposed the Caribbean Basin initiative in the summer of 1981 to assist the countries of Central America and the Caribbean in their development efforts. Colombia joined the initiative in spring of 1982. Mexico and Venezuela have accorded credit for petroleum sales, Canada increased its five year bilateral aid target for the region by over half-a-billion dollars, and Colombia has made available trade credits and preferences.

c) *General Problems Related to Preferential Arrangements*

3.118. Export expansion, insomuch as this expands LDC purchasing power has benefits to OECD exporters, although it may also increase competition facing OECD producers of some agricultural and non-agricultural products (e.g. textiles). The need to give preferential treatment to LDCs in order to aid their trade expansion is a well-established principle, reflected in a number of multilateral and national schemes. Many of the countries who have gained the most from some of these measures are the richer or more advanced developing countries who have been able to capitalise on the opportunities which they provide. In other cases, the difficulties that some of the poorest countries have experienced in expanding trade seem largely to relate not to a question of access to markets but problems in expanding supply sufficiently to take advantage of market opportunities. Therefore "supply assistance" – e.g. through development assistance targeted towards the poorest LDCs – is a necessary adjunct to these schemes.

IV. NON-AGRICULTURAL POLICIES AND THEIR EFFECT ON OECD-LDC AGRICULTURAL TRADE

3.119. Agricultural trade issues and problems between OECD members and LDCs must be viewed in the broader perspective of world trade and development. Earlier sections of this chapter stressed the importance of the interdependence of countries in world agricultural trade. Agricultural policy actions – either domestic or trade actions – of one country will have implications for other countries and a prerequisite for any improvement in the world trading system is that these interdependencies are recognised and understood by national policymakers.

3.120. Another important aspect of this interdependence is the interaction between agriculture and other sectors of the national and world economy. The policies and events in the industrial, transportation and commercial sectors of individual economies have an effect on and are affected by the policies and events in the agricultural sectors. This interaction spills over into the world market and thus has an impact on trade.

3.121. This section considers some of the aspects of this interaction which are of particular significance to OECD-LDC agricultural trade. This discussion is divided into three sections: OECD Policies; LDC Policies; and Multilateral Initiatives.

A. OECD Policies

3.122. Access to OECD agricultural markets provides a means to stimulate LDC growth and to sustain the expansion of demand for OECD agricultural exports within LDCs themselves. Access to OECD industrial and consumer goods markets is even more important for the LDCs. The domestic market for industrial products within most LDCs is not large enough to sustain the development and growth of many manufacturing enterprises. Access to foreign markets – especially the large OECD markets – is necessary in order for these enterprises to be successful. Indeed, the secret of success for most of the NICs has been the development of export-oriented consumer goods industries.

3.123. The importance of LDCs both as sources and as markets for OECD trade in manufactures relative to trade in food is shown in Table 3.13. LDC markets accounted for 25.1 per cent of total OECD manufactured exports in 1980 (shown at the top of the Table) and had a composite growth rate of 10.5 per cent over the 1972-80 period. This compares with a 68.4 per cent share associated with intra-OECD trade and a 5.1 per cent growth rate. Just as in agricultural trade, LDCs are the leading source of growth in OECD manufactured exports and the NICs and OPEC are the fastest growing LDC markets.

3.124. The transition occurring in LDC economies – as well as in the structure of world trade – is better illustrated in the import section at the bottom of Table 3.13 which shows the sources of OECD imports and their rates of growth. Manufactured products from LDCs still accounted for less than 10 per cent of OECD imports in 1980 compared with a 29 per cent LDC share of OECD food imports, but the rate of growth of OECD imports of LDC manufactures was 12.3 per cent compared with only a 5.3 per cent increase in manufactured imports from OECD sources.

3.125. The seven newly industrialised countries accounted for 6.3 per cent of OECD manufactured imports in 1980 and OECD countries increased their imports from the NICs at an annual average rate of 17.5 per cent between 1972 and 1980. OECD manufactured imports from the other groups of LDCs grew at rates equal to or greater than the average of all

Table 3.13

COMPARISON OF FOOD AND MANUFACTURING EXPORTS AND IMPORTS OF THE OECD

Destination	Food (1) Share 1980 (4)	Food (1) Growth 1972-80 (5)	Manufacturing (2) Share 1980 (4)	Manufacturing (2) Growth 1972-80 (5)	All Products (3) Share 1980 (4)	All Products (3) Growth 1972-80 (5)
Exports						
OECD	65.7	4.1	68.4	5.1	70.2	4.9
CEP	7.0	14.0	3.7	7.2	3.9	6.8
LDCs	24.7	11.9	25.1	10.5	23.3	10.0
OPEC	8.3	19.7	9.0	18.0	8.2	17.3
NICs (6)	5.8	17.4	7.5	10.3	6.8	10.2
Poorest LDCs (7)	4.6	9.5	3.7	6.9	3.6	6.7
Other LDCs	6.0	5.6	4.8	6.6	4.7	5.9
World (8)	100.0	6.1	100.0	6.3	100.0	5.9
Imports						
OECD	66.1	3.6	86.2	5.3	64.8	2.1
CPE	1.9	-4.2	2.2	6.6	3.4	6.1
LDCs	29.3	3.6	9.9	12.3	29.9	10.8
OPEC	2.2	5.3	.4	15.4	17.2	18.2
NICs (6)	9.6	3.7	6.3	17.5	5.7	9.5
Poorest LDCs (7)	7.6	4.1	1.0	8.8	3.6	6.9
Other LDCs	9.9	3.6	2.2	5.9	3.4	1.4
World (8)	100.0	3.2	100.0	5.9	100.0	4.2

1. These columns include SITC classifications 0 + 1 + 22 + 4.
2. These columns include SITC classifications 5-8.
3. These columns include SITC classifications 0-9.
4. 1980 share of OECD exports.
5. Average annual growth rate 1972-1980 in real (inflation-adjusted) exports.
6. Includes Argentina, Brazil, Mexico, Hong Kong, South Korea, Singapore and Taiwan.
7. Countries in which the per capita GDP was below $500 in 1977 (UNCTAD definition).
8. Including countries not listed above, i.e. other developed, non-OECD countries.

Note: OECD includes Yugoslavia and Intra-EEC trade.

Source: OECD Statistics of Foreign Trade, Series C.

OECD imports (5.9 per cent) but their combined market shares accounted for only 3.6 per cent of OECD manufactured imports in 1980.

3.126. The growth of OECD-LDC trade in manufactures has clearly been an engine of growth in the past decade. Yet despite this performance, the International Monetary Fund reported recently that, the loss of dynamism in world trade has been particularly marked in the case of manufactured products "...The growth of world exports of manufactures decelerated from 11 per cent annually during 1963-1973 to 5 per cent during 1974-1980, and further to 3 per cent in 1981. In the past 18-24 months, a few existing import restrictions were liberalised, but in the main the trend was toward increased protective actions that affected not only historically protected industries, but also new sectors"[64]. This trend has serious implications for world agricultural trade since it is the earnings from manufactured exports which has fueled much of the growth in LDC agricultural imports.

3.127. It was shown in Chapter II that the income elasticity of demand for food is greater in LDCs than in OECD countries (see Table 2.26). Hence, an increase in LDC export earnings is likely to generate more food import demand from LDCs than a similar export earnings increase in OECD countries. An increase in OECD trade restrictions on manufactured goods, particularly LDC exports, will therefore have a negative effect on OECD agricultural exports because of their impact on LDCs' export earnings.

3.128. OECD macro-economic policies which affect the growth of OECD markets will have the same effect on OECD agricultural exports. Policies which result in a slowdown of general economic growth decrease import demand which, in turn, reduces the ability of other countries to import. The growth in demand for agricultural products may be affected very little by a downturn in economic activity in OECD countres but slow world economic growth will have a substantial dampening effect on the expansion of food demand in LDCs – the major growth market for agricultural exports.

B. Developing Countries' Policies

3.129. Non-agricultural LDC measures which affect OECD-LDC agricultural trade fall into two major categories: financial policies and industrial development policies. The first set includes exchange rate policies and problems which have arisen from financing development from external sources.

3.130. Exchange rates can have major trade distorting effects when they are managed by governments in a way that causes the official value of a currency to deviate widely from its purchasing power vis-à-vis that of other currencies. An overvalued exchange rate discourages exports since importing countries must pay higher prices for a particular good than they would if they imported it from a different source. An undervalued exchange rate has the opposite effect.

3.131. According to the IMF, 43 members of the Fund maintained multiple currency practices at the end of March 1982[65]. Thirty-five of these countries were LDCs while only three were OECD members. Many LDCs use multiple exchange rates to favour the export of processed products over unprocessed commodities. A recent study estimated for the agricultural sector, that a mutual reduction in developed country tariff escalation *and* in LDC exchange rate and tax bias against less processed commodity exports would yield a 1.1 billion dollar per annum increase in the value of LDC exports of seven commodities (copra, rubber, cocoa, cotton, wood, leather and coffee)[66].

3.132. The decline in commodity prices and the widening world recession in the past year has reduced the revenues earned from trade for many of the LDCs. A number of these countries which had high levels of external debt are finding it increasingly difficult to make the payments due on that debt. The IMF reported that, "... External payments arrears incurred by Fund members rose sharply in the late 1970s but have since levelled off at close to SDR 5.4 billion in 1981. The number of Fund members incurring arrears, however, continued to increase steadily – more than doubling from 1975 to 1981, from 15 to 32 countries"...[67].

3.133. These financial difficulties pose a less serious threat to LDC basic food imports since reductions in imports will probably be made in the non-food areas first (given that existing contracts must be honoured). However, they do pose a threat to higher value, less essential agricultural imports in two ways. First, debt problems may result in higher levels of protection on "unessential" agricultural products. Second, and perhaps more significant higher levels of protection and other restrictions on all products and sectors of the economy may limit economic growth which, in turn, will slow the growth in demand, for example, for meat and dairy products as well as for feedstuffs.

3.134. The second set of non-agricultural developments policies which have a significant effect on OECD-LDC agricultural trade are the general macroeconomic development policies pursued by individual LDCs. One of the most important is the level of protection for industrial products because many of these are inputs in the development of a more efficient, technically advanced agricultural sector. Table 3.7 compared ad valorem tariff rates for selected LDCs for agricultural, industrial and total product groupings. In 13 of 35 countries the tariffs on imports of industrial products were about 30 per cent. Most of these countries had similar or higher average rates of protection for the agricultural sector. India, Bangladesh and Pakistan had the highest levels of protection with total average rates between 70 and 76 per cent. These high rates of protection indicate a policy designed to achieve self-sufficiency in all sectors of the economy. High tariffs may work to the net benefit of one or a few industries, but the long-term efficiency of most sectors of the economy will suffer as a result.

3.135. Policies towards industrial development also affect agriculture through their impact on labour markets. A rapidly expanding industrial sector and the resultant generation of job opportunities – especially for unskilled workers – helps to ease the pressure of population on the land in rural areas. However, industrial growth and development without concurrent development in the agricultural sector can generate a "dual economy" where the rural areas are backward and poverty-stricken and the urban areas are modern, industrial and affluent. There is a dichotomy between the living standards of rural and urban populations in most countries but the divisions are more pronounced in the LDCs. Policies which promote industrial development do little to transform conditions in rural areas unless they are coupled with measures directed at the rural areas themselves. The Brazilian experience with the backward Northeast rural areas over the past 15 years is a testament to the difficulty in finding an appropriate solution to rural problems.

3.136. Government investment in transportation and storage facilities as well as in other structural and institutional facilities to service the agricultural sector is of immense importance in many LDCs. Price incentives have little effect if the transportation costs from the producer to the point of consumption are far greater than the transport costs from alternative supply sources in other countries.

3.137. These macroeconomic policies all have a common thread – they affect the relationship between rural farming and urban industrial sectors in LDCs. This relationship and how it develops in different countries influences both the level of food import demand (or export supply) in each country as well as the mix of products imported (or exported). A better integration of the rural and urban economies in LDCs will generate faster and more even income growth which will result in greater demand for high value food products such as meat and dairy products. Some LDCs may be able to meet the growing demand for these products from domestic sources but most are likely to require at least some imports of animal feed and of the products themselves.

3.138. A more thorough integration of the rural and urban economies in LDCs will help stabilise world agricultural markets – other things held constant – because it will allow more interaction between producers and consumers in the domestic economy. To a large extent, world market prices changes are not transmitted to rural areas in LDCs because of poor infrastructure. Likewise, the food needs of large urban areas in LDCs are often filled by external sources simply because the domestic food marketing structure cannot meet urban requirements. Better integration of the rural and urban sectors would mean that many of the changes in supply or demand in an individual country would be resolved within the country itself before spilling over onto the world market.

C. Multilateral Policies and Practices

3.139. Many of the international conventions and initiatives which deal specifically with agriculture that were discussed in section III B are merely specific parts of broader measures to address the problems of trade and development. This section will elaborate on some of these broader initiatives and their objectives.

3.140. The world trading system since the end of World War II has been based on the principles established in the General Agreements on Tariffs and Trade (GATT). The central tenet of this legal trading framework is that a tariff reduction and other preferential benefits negotiated between two countries automatically applies to all other participants. In addition, all tariff reductions negotiated under the auspices of the GATT are bound at the agreed level, i.e. they cannot exceed the negotiated levels.

3.141. A number of changes have been made – if not in the philosophy at least in the practice of this trading framework. One change, which has been significant for LDCs, is the emergence of preferential arrangements which include the General Systems of Preferences, the Lomé Convention and more recently, the U.S. Caribbean Basin initiative. These are significant because they provide for non-reciprocal tariff reductions by developed countries for LDCs. Tariff concessions under these arrangements, however, are not bound and can be terminated unilaterally by the implementing country. Also the concessions are often circumscribed by product exclusions, quotas and other limitations. Hence, the legal framework suggests that the whole tariff preference system is intended to be temporary and that, as LDCs – individually or as a group – become more competitive on world markets, these preferences will be phased out.

3.142. This phasing out has, in a sense, already begun. The Tokyo Round negotiations resulted in a greater proportional reduction in MFN rates than in GSP rates. GSP tariff rates are therefore somewhat less advantageous to LDCs (relative to MFN rates) when compared with the pre-Tokyo Round tariffs. Further multilateral efforts to reduce trade barriers may well have the same result. In the future therefore many LDCs – especially the newly industrialised countries – may have more to gain in trade discussions by negotiating on a receiprocal basis.

3.143. Trade liberalisation in all products – not just products currently of interest to LDCs – is of utmost importance to a global economic development. The development process itself requires a transformation of a country's economy and its export products. Reduction of trade barriers in tropical products, for example, may not be as advantageous for long term development as a reduction of barriers to trade in light manufactured products which will stimulate the diversification of LDC economies. The trade liberalisation mechanisms established through GATT can be used to achieve this objective but it will require the participation (and treatment) of LDCs as equal partners.

3.144. Textiles are an important product area in this respect because the high labour content in the production of clothing allows LDCs with low cost semi-skilled labour to compete on world markets with many of the industrialised countries. The Multi-Fibre Arrangement, negotiated under GATT auspices, governs much of the current world trade in textiles. The Arrangement "... requires that any restrictions imposed must permit exports from an affected supplying country to expand in an orderly and equitable manner..."[68]. The result has been a number of bilateral agreements in which the exporting country agreed to limit its exports. As a multilateral agreement, the MFA has controlled unilateral initiatives to restrict imports and has allowed exporting countries continued, but often restricted, access to major markets. It has benefited exporting countries because quota restrictions have allowed them to upgrade the quality (and value) of their exports to the restricted markets without the threat of losing market share to other exporting countries. It has, however, tended to prevent new low cost exporters from gaining access to important consumer markets. In this sense it has been an impediment to development.

3.145. The developing countries have much at stake in the current concern about the health of the international trading system. Due to the great diversity in the stage of development and resource availability of individual developing countries, the benefits which each country may reap from a more open trading system vary widely. Already the pace of development of some economies – notably the NICs – have been stimulated by their more open trading policies. On the other hand, benefits accruing to the poorest LDCs are correspondingly less: these countries may continue to need specific assistance from the OECD countries. Nevertheless it is in the mutual interests of all trading partners – developed or developing – to promote a more open system of agricultural trade. OECD countries must be willing participants and must recognise the benefits which they themselves will receive from an expanding trade with countries whose populations are experiencing a rapid growth in incomes.

Chapter IV

POLICY IMPLICATIONS OF THE DEVELOPMENT OF OECD AGRICULTURAL TRADE WITH DEVELOPING COUNTRIES

4.1. The previous chapters of this report have stressed the interdependence between the economies of the developing countries and the OECD countries and have outlined various bilateral and multilateral institutions which promote trade between these two groups. Partially as a result of these institutions and measures which favourise their two-way trade, the rate of increase in OECD exports of both food and agricultural raw materials to this group has exceeded the rate of growth of exports to the world as a whole (including intra-OECD trade). The growth in exports to LDCs has been particularly strong for feedgrains, oilseeds, meat and live animals and fruits and vegetables i.e. those products whose consumption tends to be more sensitive to the growth in income. The developing countries as a group now account for roughly one-quarter of the OECD's total food and agricultural raw material exports or roughly U.S. $46 billion worth of products in 1980.

4.2. On the import side of the picture, the OECD area continues to be a major importer of LDC agricultural products. In 1980 these totalled roughly $58 billion. The rate of increase in OECD imports of food and agricultural raw materials from LDCs has exceeded the rate of growth in imports from the world as a whole (including intra-OECD trade). Growth in imports has been most rapid in some of the higher income products such as oilseeds and meals (for feed) and fruit and vegetables. The OECD continues to be a major importer of important LDC agricultural exports, tropical beverages, spices, and sugar.

4.3. The expansion of agricultural trade has important implications for the agricultural sectors of both groups of countries. It also has implications for the national and multilateral policies which provide the framework for trade. In the following sections the general implications of the expansion in trade are summarised and the particular implications for policy-makers in the OECD countries are explored.

I. GENERAL IMPLICATIONS OF THE DEVELOPMENT OF TRADE

4.4. The analysis in this report has indicated the differences which exist among the LDCs in terms of the nature of their agricultural trade with the OECD area and how this has been changing over time. These differences are due to the influence of structural economic factors and policies both in the OECD area and in the LDCs themselves.

4.5. For some LDCs, the OECD is still largely a market for agricultural exports, although considerable diversity exists in the nature of the exported products and their relationship to

OECD agriculture. Some LDCs primarily supply products which do not compete (or compete to only a limited extent) with those produced by OECD agriculture e.g. tropical beverages and such industrial raw materials as natural rubber. Others supply products which compete directly with those produced in the OECD area e.g. animal feedingstuffs, fruits and vegetables. Considerable diversity also exists in the form in which these products are supplied for example, unprocessed, lightly processed or highly processed. For other LDCs, the OECD is largely a source of agricultural imports. Again, considerable diversity exists, with situations ranging from one in which imports from the OECD are composed primarily of basic foodgrains to those in which they are dominated by higher income products such as meat or feedgrains.

4.6. Such diversity implies that a single set of relationships between the OECD and LDCs in the area of agricultural trade does not exist. Rather, there is a whole spectrum of relationships, with differences both on the export and the import side, which reflects the substantial economic diversity among the LDCs themselves. This *diversity of the LDCs* both in terms of the nature of their agricultural trade with the OECD and more generally in terms of their overall economic structure implies that differences exist in their policy concerns and needs with respect to agricultural trade.

4.7. Despite the diversity in the structure and role of trade in the LDCs, there are a number of *shared LDC concerns* with respect to agricultural trade. As exporters, LDCs are all concerned with maintaining access to overseas markets, reducing the barriers to trade that they face, and ensuring that excessive and unpredictable fluctuations in export earnings are controlled. As importers, all developing countries have substantial interest in the promotion of food security through trade as well as self-sufficiency (food security) through increased domestic production. The developmental aspect is especially important for the food security of the poorest LDCs which can help to maintain the level of food imports at a sustainable volume in terms of their foreign earnings capacity, and to ensure the continued viability of relatively less-monetized rural areas. For the industrialising LDCs, it may focus on the question of ensuring a dependable supply of imported food at dependable prices.

4.8. In assessing current policies relating to OECD/LDC agricultural trade and more particularly in framing new policies, it is necessary to take into account the common or shared concerns of the LDCs and at the same time the important structural differences within the group. The LDCs are not a homogeneous entity and policies which recognise these differences may be needed both by the LDCs and the OECD to deal with problems affecting their agricultural trading relationship. The gains accruing to each group of countries (and to individual countries within each group) will of course vary according to their stages of economic development and ability to participate in the international market.

4.9. The expansion of agricultural trade between the OECD area and the LDCs provides considerable benefits for both groups of countries. *The benefits of expanded trade* accrue to both groups in the form of gains in economic efficiency through better allocation of resources and the contribution that this makes to the growth in national income, farm sector income and export earnings, the level of food consumption, and the diversity and quality of the diet. For both sets of countries the expansion of trade permits the natural exploitation of comparative advantage, although the rate of expansion is governed by demand conditions and is influenced by the policies pursued by the two groups. The increasing volume of trade is a reflection of the fact that both groups gain from trade and that, given current production and consumption conditions, more can be gained through trade than through policies of self-sufficiency practised by individual countries.

4.10. This is an important principle, particularly from the perspective of policy, since there is sometimes a tendency to view increases in food imports by LDCs as a negative factor i.e. as an indicator that the domestic agricultural sector and the economy of LDCs is inadequate or failing. However, in many LDCs, particularly those which have been industrialising rapidly, the increasing volume of food imports and the reduction of self-sufficiency in food is a reflection of the success of the domestic economy and of their development strategy. Such countries have exploited their comparative advantage in the production of non-agricultural goods and through trade have succeeded in improving the diet and standard of living of their people. In other countries, particularly some of the poorest LDCs, rising food imports are a reflection of general economic difficulties created by low agricultural productivity per capita, the effects of policies which contribute to an imbalance between domestic demand and supply, and the lack of sufficient exports of agricultural or non-agricultural products to sustain food imports. For these two types of countries the reasons for the rise in food imports are different, the implications of increasing imports are different, and the policy approaches to imports should also be different.

4.11. For the richer developing countries, it is important that mutually beneficial agricultural trade with the OECD area continue to expand. Policies of both the LDCs themselves and of the OECD countries should be designed to contribute to this expansion and to the future stability of the trading relationship. For the poorest countries, the need is to correct the domestic economic problems that foster the reliance on high levels of imports which must be purchased with limited amounts of foreign exchange. Policies in both the LDCs and the OECD countries should be designed to assist in the improvement of agricultural productivity and marketing infrastructure in poorer countries. In addition, special assistance to enable these countries to develop a sustainable position in t⸺ international trading system will be required.

4.12. In order to achieve the desired results for the different ty :s of LDCs both national and multilateral policies are of great importance. In the following sections the nature of these policies is reviewed and overall policy conclusions are derived.

II. NATIONAL POLICIES AND THE FUTURE DEVELOPMENT OF TRADE

4.13. The growth of trade in agricultural products between OECD countries and the LDCs reflects the *growing interdependence* between the economies of the two groups. The OECD is the principal source of agricultural products imported by the LDCs and at the same time the principal destination for the LDCs' own agricultural exports. This two-way relationship creates interdependency between the agricultural sectors of the two groups of countries. It implies that the domestic agricultural and agricultural trade policies pursued by each group will affect the agricultural sector of the other. This concept was highlighted in the first half of Chapter III.

4.14. This interdependency is further intensified through the trade in non-agricultural products between the two groups. The OECD is both the principal source of the manufactured goods imported by the LDCs and the principal destination for their own exports of manufactures. The economic policies pursued by one group which influence its trade in these products will have implications for trade and economic activity in the other group. Since economic interlinkage extends across both agricultural and non-agricultural products, policies which influence one set of products are likely to influence the other set. This implies that both the agricultural and non-agricultural policies pursued in the OECD area and in the LDCs will influence the future development of agricultural trade between the two groups of countries. Furthermore, a single sector or single commodity approach to trade problems may generate undesirable secondary effects for other commodities or sectors. These may limit the scope for the growth and development of the future OECD/LDC agricultural trading relationship.

4.15. Previous chapters of this study highlighted the significance of the rate of economic growth in both the OECD area and the LDCs as the underlying force behind the recent expansion of agricultural trade between the two groups. Furthermore, the substantial dependence of LDC economic growth upon economic conditions in the OECD area was indicated. As the world's largest importing region, variations in the OECD's demand for imports of both agricultural and industrial products created by variations in OECD economic activity have significant implications for export earnings and economic growth in LDC exporters. Through the interdependences indicated above, these will also have significant implications for the OECD's own exports of agricultural and non-agricultural products to the developing countries.

4.16. The rate of economic growth in the OECD area is influenced by many factors, some of which lie outside the control of most OECD countries (e.g. the price of imported energy) and some of which are largely within the control of these countries (e.g. monetary and fiscal policy). Variations in both the controllable and the uncontrollable determinants of economic activity in the OECD area will affect the future growth of total and agricultural trade between the OECD and the developing countries.

4.17. The recent experience of OECD countries with high and persistent rates of inflation has led many governments to exercise considerable caution in both fiscal and monetary policy. In the longer-term, the use of policies which contribute to the maintenance of high real interest rates would depress economic activity in the OECD area through their effects upon business profitability and investment. Reduced economic growth in OECD countries depresses their demand for imports, including agricultural imports. The reduction in demand in OECD countries affects the foreign trade earnings and income of third countries, particularly the LDCs, and ultimately the LDCs' own imports of agricultural and industrial products. Thus the use of macro-economic policies which contribute to low rates of economic growth in the OECD could have a substantial impact on the future development of OECD/LDC agricultural trade. In the future, the implementation of policies in all countries (both OECD and non-OECD) which contribute to sustainable non-inflationary growth in the world economy will be important for the renewed expansion of world trade in total, and for the continued expansion of agricultural trade between the OECD countries and the developing countries

4.18. Given the current slow rate of growth in the OECD area and the high rate of unemployment, pressure has been increasing in many countries for the restriction of those imports which are viewed as a threat to domestic employment. These pressures are being felt in both the OECD area and in LDCs and could have major implications for the future development of trade between the two groups. As this study has indicated, trade between the OECD and the LDCs is a web of interdependent relationships. The imports and exports of each group are inextricably linked together, as are the agricultural and non-agricultural components of trade. Thus the restriction of agricultural and/or non-agricultural imports from the LDCs by OECD countries in order to protect domestic industries would reduce the foreign earnings of LDCs and their rate of economic growth. This in turn would reduce the LDCs own demand for imports of agricultural and non-agricultural products from the OECD. It may also generate pressures within the LDCs to impose resrictions on imports in order to conserve foreign exchange and to protect domestic employment. The web of interlationships which promotes the expansion of economic activity in both groups of countries under the liberal trading system also serves to reduce economic activity in both sets of countries when trade is reduced.

4.19. In terms of the future development of the agricultural trading relationship between the OECD and LDCs, it is clearly important that the interrelationships between domestic policies are recognised by both groups. There is a need to exercise restraint in the use of national policies, including trade policies, that may reduce the potential expansion of trade. There is also a need for both groups to reduce existing barriers to the expansion of mutually beneficial and sustainable trade flows. In order to exploit the mutual benefits from their trading relationship, both groups will need to pursue policies which facilitate adjustment in domestic industries to changes in demand and international competitivenes. The importance of such positive adjustment policies has been stressed in recent OECD documentation[69].

4.20. The expansion of trade created by these policies will benefit both the OECD countries and the LDCs as a whole. However, in order to deal with the particular problems of the poorest LDCs there is a need for the OECD countries to be particularly sensitive to the impact of their national policies upon this group. Policies in both the OECD area and in the LDCs themselves need to be aimed at the elimination of the structural and economic problems that inhibit growth in the poorer countries. In the longer-run, the objective should be to facilitate the development of these countries as full participants in the liberal trading system with its mutual benefits.

III. MULTILATERAL POLICIES AND THE FUTURE DEVELOPMENT OF TRADE

4.21. In addition to national policy measures, the trading relationship between the OECD countries and the LDCs is influenced by mechanisms and procedures that are agreed or originate at the multilateral level. Of the greatest significance in the context of agricultural trade are those arrangements which provide the framework of rules and obligations of trade and those which relate to food security.

A. The Multilateral Framework for Rights and Obligations in Trade

4.22. In the post-war period the principal vehicle for the promotion of liberal trade has been the GATT. Based upon the principle of non-discrimination the GATT has provided a framework of regulations within which trade has developed, through which disputes between signatories could be addressed, and the progressive liberalisation of trade could be pursued. The nature of the GATT has been strongly conditioned by the perceived needs of the richer industrial countries who dominate international trade. However, as LDC trade has grown, their concerns in the international trade area have been articulated through UNCTAD and also reflected in the GATT. The concepts of non-reciprocity and preferential treatment (e.g. through the GSP) have been accepted in the GATT and particular attention has been paid to LDC concerns in recent GATT negotiations (e.g. through separate sectoral negotiations on tropical products).

4.23. The growing significance of the LDCs in the world trade system implies that it is important for them to be as fully integrated as possible into the liberal trading system and its institutions, such as GATT. At the same time, recognition needs to be made of the differences between LDCs; their different needs, and the extent to which they can be expected to implement the fundamental principles of the GATT – overall reciprocity and non-discrimination. In particular, there is a need to provide preferential treatment and minimal reciprocal obligations for the more disadvantaged, poorest LDCs.

4.24. There is an argument for the fuller integration of the more advanced developing countries into the international trading system. A broad approach can be imagined for achieving increased integration of developing countries into the international trading system, as these countries become able to assume normal rights and obligations: the acceptance by them of greater responsibilities in the area of international trade which, in the light of the high degree of competitiveness some of these countries have achieved, could be linked to the evolution of the preferential treatment from which they are now benefiting. This approach would involve adherence to and greater participation in the GATT regulations – i.e. the more active a developing country's participation, the more necessary its acceptance of GATT rules. From an agricultural perspective, this approach would allow joint concerns of developing countries and OECD countries on agricultural trade policy and market access to be brought into a more comprehensive framework. Both sides could seek access for their respective products using the concept of "give and take" concerning concessions extending over both agricultural and non-agricultural products.

4.25. The acceptance by the more advanced LDCs of the full rules and obligations of the GATT may allow for the more extensive development of preferential treatment for the poorer countries. Possible improvements to favour the poorer countries in the GSP include broader product coverage, particularly in the agricultural sector, and, for certain "sensitive" industrial products, the liberalisation of those preferential limits which still affect these countries. In the non-tariff field it might also be feasible to explore the possibility of preferential treatment for poorer LDCs. In addition, the concept of greater predictability in preferential arrangements for beneficiaries could be considered.

4.26. Experience with the GSP and related measures has indicated that improved market access alone can be insufficient to promote the development of expanding and mutually beneficial trade between OECD countries and the poorest LDCs. National and international programmes for development assistance can be used to promote the improvement of the infrastructure and the human skills necessary for such countries to benefit from the opportunities created by preferential schemes.

B. Measures to Reduce Fluctuations in Commodity Prices and the Export Earnings of Developing Countries.

4.27. A large number of developing countries rely upon exports of agricultural and other primary commodities for a significant part of their export earnings. Variability in the prices of these commodities on world markets and its effect upon the stability of export earnings gives rise to concern in developing countries and also affects their imports from trading partners, including OECD countries. As a result of their concerns, LDCs have promoted the introduction of International Commodity Agreements (ICAs) incorporating such measures as export quotas and buffer stocks in order to stabilize world primary commodity prices. Other measures to stabilize export earnings, e.g. those under the STABEX scheme of the EEC and the International Monetary Fund's compensatory financing and buffer stock facilities, have also been introduced.

4.28. Commodity Agreements in the past have had a mixed record in achieving their aims. Difficulties have sometimes arisen in reconciling competing objectives (such as price and market stability) and in obtaining sufficient financial resources to stabilise excessive fluctuations in international markets. However, if viable international agreements could be devised to stabilize the export prices of commodities of particular significance for LDCs, then these could contribute to the economic development of these countries, and to the stable expansion of the mutually beneficial trading relationship between developing countries and OECD countries. Such agreements may be of direct benefit to OECD exporters and importers of the commodities concerned or of closely related products. They may also have a role to play in stabilizing world markets for the major agricultural products of the developing countries such as foodgrains, and therefore contribute to the achievement of food security objectives discussed below. It is, however, extremely important that the objectives of such agreements be carefully developed and explicitly established, and that their technical viability be closely examined before implementation. The degree to which prices are to be influenced by an Agreement needs particularly careful assessment since there is a strong risk of impairing the resource allocating role of prices. Both producing and consuming countries have a role to play, as well as existing multilateral agencies such as the IMF, in the framing and implementation of viable agreements.

4.29. Also of great importance are compensatory financing measures aimed directly at the stabilization of export earnings. In addition to complementing international commodity agreements, these measures have a number of supplementary advantages. Most important, they can be targeted more effectively than Commodity Agreements to countries at greatest risk and in greatest need, for example, the poorest LDCs. These arrangements are of clear benefit to many developing countries and to the continued development of a mutually beneficial trading relationship between these countries and those of the OECD.

C. Food Security

4.30. The OECD countries and the LDCs share a common concern for stability and security in world food trade. This common concern has been reflected in domestic food policies and programmes e.g. food aid, as well as through multilateral institutions such as the World Food Programme, the World Food Council, International Wheat Council and the International Monetary Fund. For different countries food security is influenced by different factors. For a country which is dependent on commercial imports of food, it may relate to fluctuations in the availability and price of food in the world market or if the country's own export earnings tend to fluctuate because of world prices, to the availability of foreign exchange to purchase such food. For a country which is not primarily dependent upon commercial food imports, food insecurity may relate to fluctuations in the country's own domestic food production. There is also the long-term insecurity problem found in poorer LDCs in which domestic food production cannot meet domestic needs and sufficient foreign exchange earnings are not available to purchase food on a commercial basis[70].

4.31. Various multilateral programmes have been established to deal with each of these insecurities. International food aid through the World Food Programme is intended to deal with emergency shortfalls in food availability and to contribute to longer-term economic development. The compensatory financing scheme of the International Monetary Fund deals with export earnings fluctuations and more recently with increases in the cost of imports due to temporary reductions in domestic production or increases in world prices. These measures are supplemented by various national food aid and other programmes e.g. the EEC's food aid scheme and the PL480 programme of the U.S.

4.32. While these schemes are designed to deal with food security in individual LDCs or in the LDCs as a whole, they should be implemented in such a way that insulation of LDC food markets from international markets is minimised. Just as in the case of trade preferences, there is a need for a greater targeting of these schemes and measures in order to augment the food security of countries having the greatest need, particularly the poorest developing countries. The more economically advanced LDCs are in a better position both financially and institutionally to develop their own domestic food security programmes incorporating for example the expansion of domestic storage facilities. International assistance could be aimed at helping these countries to develop such programmes. The poorer countries could then receive the bulk of the food security assistance made available on a national or multilateral basis e.g. food aid and import financing.

4.33. In late 1982 OECD agricultural ministers: (a) "confirmed the commitment of their countries to contribute to the strengthening of world food security and (b) recognised that appropriate policies for production, prices, trade and stocks would have to be implemented by all countries concerned, both importers and exporters, and where appropriate through international commodity agreements"[71]. In this context, longer term measures such as the use of national and international assistance to improve the infrastructure for food production and distribution, policies to promote sustainable economic growth, and measures to ensure the equitable sharing of the burden of adjustment to fluctuations in world food availability are all necessary to improve world food security. Policies which improve the capacity for adjustment in the world food system and provide the maximum assistance to those countries which are least able to bear the burden of adjustment will further the mutual realisation of the shared food security aims of both the LDCs and the OECD countries.

IV. CONCLUDING OBSERVATIONS

4.34. In spite of occasional strains to the system, on balance, agricultural trade between the OECD area and the developing countries has risen dramatically since the early 1970s and has proved mutually beneficial to both groups of countries. In order to continue to foster these trade flows and, more importantly, to realise further benefits through such trade, national and multinational policies and institutions need to emphasise the continued development of their trading relationship, and at the same time deal with the particular concerns of the LDCs such as export earnings stability and food security, and also with the special problems of the poorest countries.

4.35. The growing interdependence between the economies of the OECD countries and the developing nations created by the expansion of trade implies that the economic policies pursued by each group are increasingly important for the other. The implementation of policies with narrow sectoral or commodity objectives by either group may have important implications for the other, and ultimately for the country pursuing the sectoral objective. The web of interrelationships in both agricultural and non-agricultural trade between the OECD and developing countries requires that considerable caution be exercised by each group in the formation of national policies affecting trade.

4.36. The existing national and multinational institutions which provide a variety of trade preferences to the developing countries as a group have stimulated agricultural trade and some of the more advanced developing countries (assisted also by their stronger economies) have benefitted considerably from the expansion of trade within their liberal trading system. As their development progresses, there is an argument for the fuller integration of these countries into the institutional rules and obligations of international trade. There is also an argument that preferential treatment might be adapted to the stage of development of the more advanced developing countries, at the same time recognising the needs of the poorer group of countries. A more active participation of developing countries in the GATT would allow joint concerns of LDCs and OECD countries on agricultural trade policy and market access to be brought into a more comprehensive framework.

Appendix:

DATA AND METHODS

A. DATA SOURCES, DEFINITIONS AND COUNTRY COVERAGE

No single, comprehensive data series was available for a sufficiently long time period to permit both the longer term trend analysis of world trade in Chapter I and the shorter term analysis of trade flows in Chapter II. Consequently two sets of data were used. To the maximum extent possible, commodity coverage and country definitions were made consistent between the two sets. In general, the commodity coverage used in Chapter II is more comprehensive than data used for the analysis in Chapter I. Country definitions are given in Table A.1 and details of commodity coverage are in Table A.2.

The principal source of data for Chapter I was the *FAO Trade Yearbook*, the *Yearbook of Forest Products*, the *Production Yearbook* and the *U.N. Statistical Yearbook*. The principal sources used in Chapter II were the *OECD Series C Trade Statistics by Source and Destination*, the UNCTAD *Handbook on International Trade and Development Statistics*, *FAO Trade Yearbook*, and statistics from the World Bank's *1982 Development Report*.

Table A.1

INTRA-TRADE OF THE EC RELATIVE TO WORLD AND OECD TRADE IN SELECTED PRODUCTS.

	\multicolumn{6}{c}{EC intra-trade as a percentage of}
	World imports		OECD exports		OECD imports	
	1974	1980	1974	1980	1974	1980
Meat	50.4	45.7	66.0	57.6	68.5	70.4
Dairy products	39.8	35.2	47.7	37.1	55.0	65.8
Foodgrains and products	8.6	5.5	12.2	7.0	34.9	30.7
Feedgrains	14.0	9.1	18.7	10.3	20.7	19.7
Sugar	6.1	4.4	30.7	14.2	9.5	11.4

Source: FAO and EUROSTAT.

Table A.2

REGIONAL GROUPINGS USED FOR ANALYSIS

OECD and Yugoslavia
- -- European Community (9 Members)
- -- European Free Trade Association (EFTA)
- -- Other Western Europe (Turkey, Yugoslavia, Spain, Greece)
- -- Canada
- -- United States
- -- Japan
- -- Australia and New Zealand

Other Developed Market Economies (Israel, South Africa, Gibraltar, Malta, Faeroe Islands.)

Centrally Planned Economies (CPE)

Less Developed Countries
- -- Less Developed Africa (All African countries except South Africa)
- -- North Africa (African countries on the Mediterranean Sea plus Sudan, Spanish Sahara, Mauritania, Mali, Niger and Chad)
- -- Sub-Saharan Africa -- Africa excluding the North African countries and South Africa
- -- Latin America (All countries in Latin America including Cuba)
- -- West Asia (All Asian countries west of Pakistan including Cyprus and excluding Turkey)
- -- East Asia (Pakistan and all Asian countries to the east excluding Japan and Asian Centrally planned Countries)
- -- Less Developed Oceania (All countries in Oceania excluding Australia and New Zealand)
- -- OPEC -- Member countries of the Organization of Petroleum Exporting Countries
- -- Newly Industrialised Countries (Mexico, Brazil, Argentina, Hong Kong, Taiwan, S. Korea and Singapore)
- -- Least Developed Countries (Countries with per capita GDP below $500 in 1977)

B. NOTES ON METHODS FOR CHAPTER I

1. General

Commodities were chosen for inclusion in the analysis on the basis of their significance in world trade. Commodities were included if the world value of imports in 1980 was greater than $2 billion. Some exceptions were made to this rule in order to ensure completeness in aggregation or to prevent the omission of a commodity group, e.g. vegetables. Some commodities which met the significance criteria had to be excluded because of the lack of sufficiently long data series, e.g. cattle.

Quantities of world imports by commodity were aggregate into groups using 1969-71 average world unit imports values as weights. The weighted aggregates were then converted to index numbers (1969-71 = 100). The choice of imports as the indicator of world trade is arbitrary, world exports could have been used as an alternative. Although some differences exist between recorded exports and imports in the FAO series due to loss, shrinkage and accounting problems, such differences would not be significant at the level of aggregation used in the study.

Table A.3

COMMODITIES INCLUDED IN THE STUDY

Commodity Group	Product Composition (SITC codes)			
	Chapter I		Chapter II	
Foodgrains and products	041	-- Wheat	Those in Chapter I plus	
	042	-- Rice	047	-- Other cereal flours/meals
	046	-- Wheat flour	048	-- Cereal preparations
Feedgrains and substitutes	043	-- Unmilled barley	Those in Chapter I plus	
	044	-- Unmilled maize	045	-- Unmilled other cereals
			081	-- Feeds and fodder less oilseed meals (0813)
Oilseeds and products	2222	-- Soyabeans	05481	-- Cassava, arrowroot etc.
	4232	-- Soyabean oil	022	-- Oilseeds
	4242	-- Palm oil	0813	-- Oilseed meals
	08131	-- Soyabean cake		
Dairy products	02232/43	-- Milk and cream dry	02	-- Dairy products and eggs
	023	-- Butter		
	024	-- Cheese and curd		
Meat	0111	-- Meat of bovine animals	00	-- Live animals
	0112	-- Meat of sheep and goats	01	-- Meat and meat preparations
	0113	-- Pigmeat		
	0114	-- Poultrymeat		
Fruit	0571	-- Oranges, tangerines	Aggregated with vegetables	
	0573	-- Bananas		
	0574	-- Apples	05	-- Vegetables and fruit (less 05481)
Vegetables	0541	-- Potatoes	Aggregated with fruit above	
	0542	-- Pulses	See fruit above	
Sugar	0611	-- Raw centrifugal	06	-- Sugar, sugar preparations and honey
	0612	-- Refined		
Tropical beverages	0711	-- Coffee	07	-- Coffee, tea, cocoa and spices
	0721	-- Cocoa beans		
	0741	-- Tea		
Agricultural raw materials	232	-- Natural rubber	21	-- Hides and skins
	2631	-- Cotton lint	23	-- Crude rubber
	2681	-- Wool greasy	24	-- Cork and wood
	2682	-- Wool degreased	25	-- Pulp and paper
	245 + 246 + 247	-- Roundwood	26	-- Textiles and fibres
	248	-- Sawnwood and sleepers	29	-- Crude animal and vegetable materials
	251	-- Wood pulp		
	641	-- Paper and paperboard		
Agricultural products	Sum of above commodities		00	-- Food and live animals
			01	-- Beverages and tobacco
			22	-- Oilseeds and oleaginous fruits
			04	-- Animal and vegetable oils, fats and waxes

Quantities of imports and exports of each commodity for 1967-80 were extracted from the data for the following FAO-defined aggregates: Development Market Economies (DMEs), Developing Market Economies (LDMEs), Centrally Planned Economies (CPEs). Data were also extracted for Israel, Malta, South Africa and Turkey. From these, regional *commodity* aggregates were created using 1969-71 world unit import or export values (as appropriate) as weights. These were then divided by corresponding world totals to produce trade shares.

2. Analysis of Trends and Fluctuations

Trends in the total volume and regional shares of trade were analysed by fitting trend lines through ordinary least-squares (OLS) or generalised least-squares (GLS) regression. The GLS estimator was used to correct for serial correlation of residuals. The specification of functional form was based upon an inspection of plots of the data and post-estimation analysis of goodness of fit. A trend line was used in the analysis if the time coefficient (at least one of the two in the case of the quadratic function) was statistically significantly different from zero at the 5 per cent confidence level (two-tailed test). If this criterion was not satisfied for any trend line fitted, it was then assumed that no trend existed over the period. With the exception of total imports of dairy products (quadratic) and total imports of oilseeds and products (semi-logarithmic) all trend lines used in the analysis were linear.

Growth rates used in the chapter are compound rates computed from the predicted values from the trend lines. Variability is computed as the average absolute deviation from trend (arithmetic mean where no trend exists). Unless otherwise indicated, the coefficient of variation is computed by dividing the average absolute variation by the mean of the data series.

3. Implications of Including EEC Intra-Trade in the Data Used for Analysis

In the analysis of long-term trends, it is important to avoid discontinuity in the data series. Such discontinuity would have been generated in the data used in the chapter if intra-EEC trade had been excluded, particularly after the enlargement of the EEC in 1973.

In order to avoid the discontinuity created by this exclusion, the data could have been made homogeneous by excluding trade between the new members and between the old EC6 and the new entrants for the entire period of the analysis. Apart from the doubtful logic of this procedure it would have required a major effort in terms of data collection and processing. Alternatively, statistical techniques e.g. "dummy variables" could have been employed to reduce the effects of the discontinuity created by the removal of the expanded intra-trade after 1973. Given the 5 year period of transition to EEC agricultural regulations by the new entrants this procedure would not be straightforward. Furthermore the adjustment of the basic data to remove intra-trade after 1973 would require a considerable amount of processing, given differences in accounting conventions from those employed by the Community. For these reasons, EEC intra-trade was included in the analysis as part of world trade.

Some indication of the effects of this inclusion can be gained from Table A.3. For selected commodities this gives EEC9 intra-trade as a percentage of total world trade (imports), OECD exports and OECD imports in the years 1974 and 1980. Developments in EEC9 trade during this period are particularly important because of the weight placed upon recent years in deriving the trends used in this report. The commodities selected are those for which broadly comparable data to that used in this study are available, and also those which because of their importance in world and OECD trade are highly significant for the results of the study.

Since the data only relate to two years they must be interpreted with care. Because of the short time period involved it is not possible to derive meaningful trend values such as those used in the chapter. The shares presented are used as indicators of relative changes, and should not be taken as precise measurements of the magnitude of such changes.

The following observations can be made from the table:

a) Since the ratios suggest that the proportion of world imports represented by EEC intra-trade has tended to *decline*, the inclusion of this trade in the world trade data used in the chapter will tend to *understate* the historical rates of growth in world trade, excluding EEC intra-trade.

b) Since EEC intra-trade as a proportion of OECD exports has tended to *decline*, the inclusion of this trade will tend to *reduce* the historical *rates* of increase in the OECD's share of world exports of these commodities in world trade, implied by the data used in the chapter. It's impact on the *absolute value* of the OECD share of world exports cannot be determined without explicit re-calculation.

c) For meat, dairy products and sugar, since EEC intra-trade as a proportion of OECD imports has tended to *increase*, the inclusion of this trade will tend to reduce the historical rates of decline in the OECD's share of these commodities in world trade, implied by the data used in this chapter. Since the opposite relationship holds for cereals, the historical rate of decline in the OECD's share may be overstated. As in (b) above, the impact of the exclusion of EEC intra-trade upon the absolute value of the OECD's import share cannot be determined without explicit re-calculation.

NOTES AND METHODS FOR CHAPTER II

A. THE USAGE OF TRADE FLOW STATISTICS

Chapter II considers inter-country trade flows, which requires a data series which provides sources and destinations of agricultural imports and exports by countries. The *OECD Series C Trade Statistics* provides this data in value terms (current U.S. dollars) for all trade originating from or destined for OECD countries. These data are supplemented, where possible, by UNCTAD trade flow data among non-OECD countries. Although value data suffer from a number of shortcomings (e.g. inflation, fluctuating exchange rates and changing relative prices) the analyses in the following sections mitigate some of the potential distortions by concentrating on two measurements of change in market structure: (1) relative market shares and (2) the annual average growth of trade adjusted for changes in unit values.

The first measurement assumes that all countries use a consistent value for the goods trade in a given time period so that trade shares are comparable among countries in a particular year. It also assumes that changes in unit values over time are the same for different countries thereby allowing a comparison of market share changes over time.

The second measurement of market change, the annual average trade growth, was constructed from price indices based on FAO and World Bank price series data for each of the agricultural product categories. These indices were used to reflect changes in the unit values of the basket of commodities and products within each category. Dividing the relevant trade flow data by these indices removed the average fluctuations in unit values, thereby providing a measurement of actual commodity flows over time. Annual percentage growth rates were then calculated based for these commodity flows and an average was taken for the time period.

A critical assumption in the second measurement is that the price index construction adequately reflects the unit value changes which have taken place within each commodity grouping and for each country's trade. For commodity groupings with relatively close substitutes or a single dominant commodity, the index provides a relatively accurate means of capturing the actual changes in commodity flows. As commodity groupings become more heterogeneous with less cross commodity substitution, prices changes within the group may diverge and the risk of possible distortion increases.

B. PRODUCT CATEGORIES

The same 9 major product categories are used as in Chapter I as well as a total agricultural trade category. The category definitions, however, are slightly different as the use of value data has allowed the aggregation of a somewhat broader range of products within each category. Table A.3 gives the major commodity breakdown by SITC code for each of the categories as well as a comparison with the aggregations in Chapter I.

C. GEOGRAPHICAL GROUPINGS

Geographical disaggregation allows for the examination of trade flows of OECD and 7 of its member country or regional components with 10 groupings of LDCs as well as with an "LDC total", a "centrally planned total" and an "other developed market economy total". The country and regional groupings are listed in Table 2.2 The primary criteria for country grouping was geographic proximity. Significant factors such as consumption preferences, agricultural production techniques and cultural ties tend to fall more easily in regional groupings than in economic or political groups. Nevertheless, three non-geographic groupings have been included – OPEC, Newly Industrialised

Countries (NICs) and Low Income Less Developed Countries (LLDCs) because countries in each of these groups have certain economic characteristics in common. In order to simplify the analysis not all of these groups will be used in the examination of export/import trends, instead, the relevant grouping will be highlighted according to the product under consideration.

D. TIME PERIOD

The nine year period – 1972 to 1980 – is used for the analysis in Chapter II: earlier OECD data are available but do not include trade statistics for New Zealand.

NOTES AND REFERENCES

1. For technical reasons, the data used in this chapter *include* intra-European Community trade. These reasons and their implications for the results presented, are discussed in the appendix and are also noted at appropriate points in the text.
2. These variability statistics and those subsequently presented in this chapter are computed net of trend. Growth rates are computed from trend lines (see data and methods appendix for details).
3. The exclusion of intra-EC trade from the data would probably increase the growth rates calculated for most products (see the data and methods appendix).
4. This table and subsequent analysis of both export and import shares is based on the period 1967-80, the longest period for which suitable data were available.
5. Shares are computed at trend to reduce the possible error associated with "a-typical" single year comparisons.
6. The OECD's share of tropical beverage exports derives from re-exports.
7. The inclusion of EEC intra-trade in the data will tend to reduce the rates of increase in the OECD's share of exports for most commodities, implied by the figures presented here (see the data and methods appendix).
8. As an overall indicator consider the ratio of annual LDC fluctuations to 1980 share at trend for all commodities, which at 0.022 is twice as large as the corresponding OECD ratio of 0.011.
9. Since the data are shares, variability will be introduced through the behaviour of other exporters, e.g. the Centrally Planned Economies. Even if some of the variability in the LDC share is created by these exporters, the variability is higher *relative* to that of the OECD, whose share is similarly affected by the behaviour of others. This observation also applies to the subsequent analysis of relative variability in import shares.
10. The method used to measure this relationship does not distinguish whether the association is between long-term (trend) changes or short-term (variability) changes. This can however be inferred by examining plots of the shares. A combination of visual interpretation and statistical analysis was employed in this and the corresponding discussion on imports.
11. An examination of the data reveals that the gain in OECD share prior to 1975 was primarily associated with a reduction in LDC share, while after 1975 it was primarily associated with a reduction in CPC share.
12. The inclusion of intra-EEC trade in the data may tend to *understate* the rate of decline in the OECD's share of world imports for meat, dairy products and sugar, and to *overstate* it for food and feedgrains (see the data and methods appendix).
13. This is not captured by the variability measure given in Table 1.2.
14. This result and the following was based on an analysis of the association between deviations from trends in the LDC imports share and deviations from trend in a corresponding index of real import prices derived from FAO data.
15. The LDC share of world sugar imports would also be significant, increasing by roughly 1 per cent of world imports per year.

16. OECD, *Economic Outlook*, Paris, July 1983, No. 33, page 149.
17. 1980 data for LDCs were not available. Tables are presented in this chapter on the percentage growth in exports and imports by various regional groupings and their export/import shares. For details on the regional definitions see the appendix to the study. Note that the percentage growth rates computed for some regions may be large because of the small volumes involved. Information on both growth rates and shares must be compared to provide a balanced picture of the changes in trade flows.
18. This aspect of LDC economies is developed more fully in Chapter III.
19. Agricultural raw materials are not included in total agricultural trade and therefore are not listed in Table 2.4 (See the Appendix Table A.3 for the definition of products).
20. USDA, *Foreign Agriculture Circular*, 'Grains", Washington, 28th June 1982, p.9.
21. For similar reasons, imports of high protein oilseed meals also rose, as is explained in the following section.
22. Excluding EEC intra-trade.
23. Though there were marked changes in the structure of trade between OECD countries and between products.
24. Re-combining butter-oil and skim milk powder.
25. UNCTAD, *Assessment of the Results of the Multilateral Trade Negotiations*, TD/B/778/Rev.1, New York, 1982, pp.22-23.
26. For the purposes of this study this category (see Appendix Table A.3) includes live animals, meat, and meat preparations.
27. UNCTAD, *op. cit.*, pp. 22-23.
28. The income elasticities in Table 2.26 were computed for the period 1960-1970 and their current magnitude is likely to be different. However, these elasticities still provide an indication of inter-regional differences. They are also useful in explaining the increases in food demand which occurred in the past – particularly in the early 1970s.
29. See GATT, *International Trade 1980/81*, Geneva.
30. OECD, *Problems of Agricultural Trade*, Paris, 1982, paragraphs 3.78. to 3.124 See also OECD *Review of Agricultural Policies, General Survey*, paragraphs 33-50, Paris, 1975.
31. *Problems of Agricultural Trade, op. cit.*, para. 3.81.
32. OECD, *The Instability of Agricultural Commodity Markets*, Paris, 1980, page 22, para. 2.56.
33. *ibid.* page 58, para. 5.31.
34. *ibid.* page 22, para. 2.56. This concept is discussed at length in Section 5 "Implications of Agricultural Policies for Market Stability", of this study: see paragraphs 5.1 – 5.54.
35. *Food Problems and Prospects in Sub-Saharan Africa: The Decade of the 1980s*, USDA/ERS, Washington, 1981, Foreign Agriculture Report No. 166.
36. Although Thailand has policies which favour urban rice consumers, Thai production of other crops – particularly maize and manioc – increased rapidly in the past in response to world price incentives.
37. *Agricultural Protection in OECD Countries: Its Cost to Less Developed Countries*, Alberto Valdes and Joachim Zietz, IFPRI, Washington, December 1980.
38. GATT, *The Tokyo Round of Multilateral Trade Negotiations*, Geneva, April 1969, p.122.
39. *The Instability of Agricultural Commodity Markets, op. cit.*
40. *Ibid.*, p.22.
41. Shei and Thompson, "Trade Restrictions and Price Stability", *American Journal of Agricultural Economics*, November 1977, pp. 628-638. This article demonstrates that trade restrictions increase the variability of prices on the world wheat market.
42. USDA, ERS, *op. cit.*
43. *Accelerated Development in Sub-Saharan Africa: An Agenda for Action*, The World Bank, Washington, 1982, p.57.
44. *Ibid.*

45. *Problems of Agricultural Trade, op. cit.*, para. 4.18. See also paras. 4.19-4.31. This topic has also been discussed at length by the OECD Group on North-South Economic Issues and by the Development Cooperation Directorate.
46. Food aid questions have been discussed extensively within the OECD and other international fora. See OECD Development Centre, *Food Aid for Development* by H. Schneider, Paris, 1978.
47. See *Food Outlook* No. 2, 22nd February 1983, FAO p.26 for details on Donor Countries.
48. *Problems of Agricultural Trade, op. cit.*, para. 4.18. See also paras. 4.19-4.31.
49. For a general reference to this Facility see paragraph 3.92.
50. Estimated by OECD Secretariat.
51. *Problems of Agricultural Trade, op. cit.*, para. 4.46. See also paragraphs 4.44 – 4.48.
52. Since its inception 71 developing countries have made 161 purchases under this programme. A majority of these purchases were made by African countries. Other countries such as OECD Members, certain COMECON countries and countries such as South Africa have also used this facility in the past.
53. Under Lomé II a separate MINEX scheme budgeted at EUA 280 million is available during 1980-84 to cover shortfalls in mineral export earnings.
54. GATT, *The Tokyo Declaration*, Geneva, 1979.
55. GATT, *What it is, What it does*, Geneva, November 1982, p.6.
56. GATT, *The Tokyo Round of Multilateral Trade Negotiations*, Geneva, April 1979, p. 122
57. *Ibid.*, p.23.
58. *Ibid.*, p.25.
59. GATT, *Ministerial Declaration*, Geneva, 29th November, 1982.
60. Most of the material used in this section was adapted from: *The Generalised System of Preferences: Review of the First Decade*, OECD, Paris, 1983.
61. *Ibid.*
62. *Protectionism Threat to International Order, the Impact on Developing Countries*, the Commonwealth Secretariat, London, 1982, p.96.
63. It should also be recognised that as economic development progresses, it is desirable that developing country markets be made more open to imports from OECD countries.
64. *Developments in International Trade Policy*, IMF Occasional Paper No. 16, Washington, November 1982.
65. IMF, *op. cit.*
66. R. Repetto; OECD Interfutures, Intermediate Results of the Interfutures research project *Distributional Aspects of North-South Trade and Aid*, July 1978.
67. IMF, *op. cit.*
68. *GATT, What It is, What it Does, op. cit.*, p.12.
69. a) OECD, *The Case for Positive Adjustment*, Paris, 1979.
    b) OECD, *The Implications of Different Means of Agricultural Income Support*, Paris, 1983.
70. As indicated in section A.2 of Chapter III, domestic LDC policies may be a contributing factor to food insecurity in this case.
71. OECD, Press Release, "Communique", PRESS/A(82)68, Paris, 3rd December 1982, para. 13.

OECD SALES AGENTS
DÉPOSITAIRES DES PUBLICATIONS DE L'OCDE

ARGENTINA – ARGENTINE
Carlos Hirsch S.R.L., Florida 165, 4° Piso (Galería Guemes)
1333 BUENOS AIRES, Tel. 33.1787.2391 y 30.7122

AUSTRALIA – AUSTRALIE
Australia and New Zealand Book Company Pty, Ltd.,
10 Aquatic Drive, Frenchs Forest, N.S.W. 2086
P.O. Box 459, BROOKVALE, N.S.W. 2100

AUSTRIA – AUTRICHE
OECD Publications and Information Center
4 Simrockstrasse 5300 Bonn (Germany). Tel. (0228) 21.60.45
Local Agent/Agent local :
Gerold and Co., Graben 31, WIEN 1. Tel. 52.22.35

BELGIUM – BELGIQUE
Jean De Lannoy, Service Publications OCDE
avenue du Roi 202, B-1060 BRUXELLES. Tel. 02/538.51.69

BRAZIL – BRÉSIL
Mestre Jou S.A., Rua Guaipa 518,
Caixa Postal 24090, 05089 SAO PAULO 10. Tel. 261.1920
Rua Senador Dantas 19 s/205-6, RIO DE JANEIRO GB.
Tel. 232.07.32

CANADA
Renouf Publishing Company Limited,
2182 ouest, rue Ste-Catherine,
MONTRÉAL, Qué. H3H 1M7. Tel. (514)937.3519
OTTAWA, Ont. K1P 5A6, 61 Sparks Street

DENMARK – DANEMARK
Munksgaard Export and Subscription Service
35, Nørre Søgade
DK 1370 KØBENHAVN K. Tel. +45.1.12.85.70

FINLAND – FINLANDE
Akateeminen Kirjakauppa
Keskuskatu 1, 00100 HELSINKI 10. Tel. 65.11.22

FRANCE
Bureau des Publications de l'OCDE,
2 rue André-Pascal, 75775 PARIS CEDEX 16. Tel. (1) 524.81.67
Principal correspondant :
13602 AIX-EN-PROVENCE : Librairie de l'Université.
Tel. 26.18.08

GERMANY – ALLEMAGNE
OECD Publications and Information Center
4 Simrockstrasse 5300 BONN Tel. (0228) 21.60.45

GREECE – GRÈCE
Librairie Kauffmann, 28 rue du Stade,
ATHÈNES 132. Tel. 322.21.60

HONG-KONG
Government Information Services,
Publications/Sales Section, Baskerville House,
2nd Floor, 22 Ice House Street

ICELAND – ISLANDE
Snaebjörn Jónsson and Co., h.f.,
Hafnarstraeti 4 and 9, P.O.B. 1131, REYKJAVIK.
Tel. 13133/14281/11936

INDIA – INDE
Oxford Book and Stationery Co. :
NEW DELHI-1, Scindia House. Tel. 45896
CALCUTTA 700016, 17 Park Street. Tel. 240832

INDONESIA – INDONÉSIE
PDIN-LIPI, P.O. Box 3065/JKT., JAKARTA, Tel. 583467

IRELAND – IRLANDE
TDC Publishers – Library Suppliers
12 North Frederick Street, DUBLIN 1 Tel. 744835-749677

ITALY – ITALIE
Libreria Commissionaria Sansoni :
Via Lamarmora 45, 50121 FIRENZE. Tel. 579751/584468
Via Bartolini 29, 20155 MILANO. Tel. 365083
Sub-depositari :
Ugo Tassi
Via A. Farnese 28, 00192 ROMA. Tel. 310590
Editrice e Libreria Herder,
Piazza Montecitorio 120, 00186 ROMA. Tel. 6794628
Costantino Ercolano, Via Generale Orsini 46, 80132 NAPOLI. Tel. 405210
Libreria Hoepli, Via Hoepli 5, 20121 MILANO. Tel. 865446
Libreria Scientifica, Dott. Lucio de Biasio "Aeiou"
Via Meravigli 16, 20123 MILANO. Tel. 807679
Libreria Zanichelli
Piazza Galvani 1/A, 40124 Bologna Tel. 237389
Libreria Lattes, Via Garibaldi 3, 10122 TORINO. Tel. 519274
La diffusione delle edizioni OCSE è inoltre assicurata dalle migliori librerie nelle città più importanti.

JAPAN – JAPON
OECD Publications and Information Center,
Landic Akasaka Bldg., 2-3-4 Akasaka,
Minato-ku, TOKYO 107 Tel. 586.2016

KOREA – CORÉE
Pan Korea Book Corporation,
P.O. Box n° 101 Kwangwhamun, SÉOUL. Tel. 72.7369

LEBANON – LIBAN
Documenta Scientifica/Redico,
Edison Building, Bliss Street, P.O. Box 5641, BEIRUT.
Tel. 354429 – 344425

MALAYSIA – MALAISIE
University of Malaya Co-operative Bookshop Ltd.
P.O. Box 1127, Jalan Pantai Baru
KUALA LUMPUR. Tel. 51425, 54058, 54361

THE NETHERLANDS – PAYS-BAS
Staatsuitgeverij, Verzendboekhandel,
Chr. Plantijnstraat 1 Postbus 20014
2500 EA S-GRAVENHAGE. Tel. nr. 070.789911
Voor bestellingen: Tel. 070.789208

NEW ZEALAND – NOUVELLE-ZÉLANDE
Publications Section,
Government Printing Office Bookshops:
AUCKLAND: Retail Bookshop: 25 Rutland Street,
Mail Orders: 85 Beach Road, Private Bag C.P.O.
HAMILTON: Retail: Ward Street,
Mail Orders, P.O. Box 857
WELLINGTON: Retail: Mulgrave Street (Head Office),
Cubacade World Trade Centre
Mail Orders: Private Bag
CHRISTCHURCH: Retail: 159 Hereford Street,
Mail Orders: Private Bag
DUNEDIN: Retail: Princes Street
Mail Order: P.O. Box 1104

NORWAY – NORVÈGE
J.G. TANUM A/S
P.O. Box 1177 Sentrum OSLO 1. Tel. (02) 80.12.60

PAKISTAN
Mirza Book Agency, 65 Shahrah Quaid-E-Azam, LAHORE 3.
Tel. 66839

PHILIPPINES
National Book Store, Inc.
Library Services Division, P.O. Box 1934, MANILA.
Tel. Nos. 49.43.06 to 09, 40.53.45, 49.45.12

PORTUGAL
Livraria Portugal, Rua do Carmo 70-74,
1117 LISBOA CODEX. Tel. 360582/3

SINGAPORE – SINGAPOUR
Information Publications Pte Ltd,
Pei-Fu Industrial Building,
24 New Industrial Road N° 02-06
SINGAPORE 1953, Tel. 2831786, 2831798

SPAIN – ESPAGNE
Mundi-Prensa Libros, S.A.
Castelló 37, Apartado 1223, MADRID-1. Tel. 275.46.55
Libreria Bosch, Ronda Universidad 11, BARCELONA 7.
Tel. 317.53.08, 317.53.58

SWEDEN – SUÈDE
AB CE Fritzes Kungl Hovbokhandel,
Box 16 356, S 103 27 STH, Regeringsgatan 12,
DS STOCKHOLM. Tel. 08/23.89.00
Subscription Agency/Abonnements:
Wennergren-Williams AB,
Box 13004, S104 25 STOCKHOLM.
Tel. 08/54.12.00

SWITZERLAND – SUISSE
OECD Publications and Information Center
4 Simrockstrasse 5300 BONN (Germany). Tel. (0228) 21.60.45
Local Agents/Agents locaux
Librairie Payot, 6 rue Grenus, 1211 GENÈVE 11. Tel. 022.31.89.50

TAIWAN – FORMOSE
Good Faith Worldwide Int'l Co., Ltd.
9th floor, No. 118, Sec. 2,
Chung Hsiao E. Road
TAIPEI. Tel. 391.7396/391.7397

THAILAND – THAILANDE
Suksit Siam Co., Ltd., 1715 Rama IV Rd,
Samyan, BANGKOK 5. Tel. 2511630

TURKEY – TURQUIE
Kültur Yayinlari Is-Türk Ltd. Sti.
Atatürk Bulvari No : 191/Kat. 21
Kavaklidere/ANKARA. Tel. 17 02 66
Dolmabahce Cad. No : 29
BESIKTAS/ISTANBUL. Tel. 60 71 88

UNITED KINGDOM – ROYAUME-UNI
H.M. Stationery Office,
P.O.B. 276, LONDON SW8 5DT.
(postal orders only)
Telephone orders: (01) 622.3316, or
49 High Holborn, LONDON WC1V 6 HB (personal callers)
Branches at: EDINBURGH, BIRMINGHAM, BRISTOL,
MANCHESTER, BELFAST.

UNITED STATES OF AMERICA – ÉTATS-UNIS
OECD Publications and Information Center, Suite 1207,
1750 Pennsylvania Ave., N.W. WASHINGTON, D.C.20006 – 4582
Tel. (202) 724.1857

VENEZUELA
Libreria del Este, Avda. F. Miranda 52, Edificio Galipan,
CARACAS 106. Tel. 32.23.01/33.26.04/31.58.38

YUGOSLAVIA – YOUGOSLAVIE
Jugoslovenska Knjiga, Knez Mihajlova 2, P.O.B. 36, BEOGRAD.
Tel. 621.992

Les commandes provenant de pays où l'OCDE n'a pas encore désigné de dépositaire peuvent être adressées à :
OCDE, Bureau des Publications, 2, rue André-Pascal, 75775 PARIS CEDEX 16.
Orders and inquiries from countries where sales agents have not yet been appointed may be sent to:
OECD, Publications Office, 2, rue André-Pascal, 75775 PARIS CEDEX 16.

OECD PUBLICATIONS, 2, rue Andre-Pascal, 75775 PARIS CEDEX 16 - No. 42857 1984
PRINTED IN FRANCE
(51 84 02 1) ISBN 92-64-12579-5